T0340896

Olmsted and Yosemite

LALH

Olmsted and Yosemite

CIVIL WAR, ABOLITION, AND

THE NATIONAL PARK IDEA

ROLF DIAMANT AND ETHAN CARR

LIBRARY OF AMERICAN LANDSCAPE HISTORY

AMHERST, MASSACHUSETTS

Library of American Landscape History
P.O. Box 1323
Amherst, MA 01004
www.lalh.org

Library of Congress Control Number: 2021947082
ISBN: 978-1-952620-34-8

Designed by Jonathan D. Lippincott
Set in Sabon

Distributed by
National Book Network
nbnbooks.com

All photographs of Yosemite Valley are from a group of thirty mammoth-plate albumen photographs by Carleton Watkins (1829–1916), 1861. Courtesy of the Billings Family Archives, The Woodstock Foundation, Inc., Woodstock, VT 05091.

Preliminary Report upon the Yosemite and Big Tree Grove reprinted from *The Papers of Frederick Law Olmsted,* vol. 5: *The California Frontier, 1863–1865,* ed. Victoria Post Ranney (Baltimore: Johns Hopkins University Press, 1990), 488–511. Extensive notes and other explanatory material are included on pp. 511–16.

CONTENTS

Olmsted and Yosemite

INTRODUCTION

THREE LANDSCAPES

If we can re-make the Government, abolish Slavery & get the
Central Park well under [way] for our descendants, we shall have
done a work worthy of the 19th century.

—Sarah Blake Sturgis Shaw, August 1861

In 1862, Oliver Wendell Holmes, the Boston doctor, writer,
and "autocrat of the breakfast table," visited the new Central Park in New York. He was in the city to retrieve his son,
Oliver Wendell Holmes Jr., recently wounded at the battle of
Antietam. Holmes commented on the sinuous pathways that
wound through the park, passing near shaded glacial outcrops
and open meadows framed by the growing grid of city streets.
"The hips and bones of Nature," he observed, "stick out here
and there in the shape of rocks which give character to the scenery. . . . The roads were fine, the sheets of water beautiful, the
swans elegant in their deportment, the grass green and as short
as a fast horse's winter coat."[1] Though it was still unfinished—
and the country was still gripped by its greatest and most violent crisis—that year more than two million people visited the

urban landscape which had been designed and built under the direction of Frederick Law Olmsted and Calvert Vaux.

While New York was opening Central Park to the public, almost eight hundred miles to the south the small coastal town of Port Royal, South Carolina, was a world apart. The flatness of the Carolina Lowcountry that spread out around Port Royal was unbroken except for island forests of moss-draped oaks and plain scrub pine. In 1852, Olmsted, then traveling through the antebellum South to report on conditions for the *New York Times,* had described the Lowcountry landscape as a "forest of pines . . . on one side, . . . on the other was a continued succession of very large fields, of rich dark soil—evidently reclaimed swamp-land—cultivated . . . in Sea Island cotton. . . . Beyond them, a flat surface of still lower land, with a silver thread of water curling through it, extended, Holland-like, to the horizon."[2] Large swaths of this vast wetland had been drained and diked at a terrible human cost by enslaved people who worked the network of plantations growing rice, indigo, and the lucrative sea cotton.

In November 1861, a year before Holmes recorded his impressions of Central Park, the Port Royal–Hilton Head region and surrounding coastal islands were seized and occupied by Federal military forces. Tens of thousands of freedpeople stayed behind as plantation owners and overseers fled to the Confederate-controlled interior. The ranks of those who remained in the Union-occupied coastal enclaves were swelled by refugees from nearby plantations seeking freedom and sanctuary. Declared by Congress as "contraband" of war, their future status as Americans was yet to be determined. But it was clear that what was happening at Port Royal and the rest of the Lowcountry was nothing less than what Lincoln would later describe in his Gettysburg Address as "a new birth of freedom."

On the other side of the continent from Central Park and Port Royal, almost three thousand miles overland and more than six thousand miles by sea and across the Isthmus of Panama, was another landscape: a deep gorge embedded in California's Sierra Nevada. The sheer verticality of Yosemite Valley set it apart from almost anywhere else on earth. Immense walls of multi-hued granite, theatrically lit by ephemeral shafts of invading sunlight, were streaked with the timeless stains of cascading waters. Unlike the exposed openness of the southeastern coastline, the forested floor of Yosemite Valley was enclosed and verdant. In the early 1850s, white settlers invaded the territory of the valley's Indigenous inhabitants, Southern Sierra Miwok, also known as the Ahwahneechee. Militiamen burned their villages and drove them from the region. Small numbers of Native people gradually returned to the valley to reestablish a tenuous existence that lasted into the early twentieth century. As travelers' descriptions and photographs of this majestic landscape made their way east in the midst of the Civil War, Congress considered the unprecedented step of setting aside Yosemite out of the public domain as a park for the people of the United States for all time.

The fate of these three landscapes—Central Park, Port Royal, and Yosemite—would become linked in unexpected ways. It can be argued that the 1864 act of Congress granting Yosemite Valley and the adjacent Mariposa Grove of giant sequoias to the State of California to be held in trust for the people of the United States was in part a consequence of the creation of New York's Central Park and in part a consequence of the social revolution taking place in Port Royal. Central Park provided the inspiration and example for public park making and scenic landscape preservation on a scale never before attempted in the nation. What was happening on the Southern Sea Islands was representative of a transformative moment in

America, when the momentum for emancipation and reconstruction would trigger a broader agenda of reforms. Those
reforms would redefine and extend the rights and benefits of
American citizenship and would come to include guaranteed
public access to places such as Yosemite. Events occurring in
each of these places—New York, South Carolina, and California—would enable the idea of national parks to gain a tenuous
but portentous foothold in America. One common thread running through them all was the peripatetic life of Frederick Law
Olmsted (1822–1903).

Best known today as a landscape architect and the codesigner
of Central Park, Olmsted, after extensive travels in the South,
served the Union during the Civil War as executive director of
the United States Sanitary Commission providing medical aid to
wounded soldiers. In 1865 he wrote a report intended to guide
the future management of Yosemite Valley as a public park and
in the process laid the intellectual foundation for a system of
national parks. During a remarkable period of national rein-
vention, Olmsted appears repeatedly, in the contexts of urban
design, scenic preservation, and social justice. Obscured over
time, these connections deserve renewed consideration today.

This book offers a fresh perspective on the creation of
national parks in the United States by connecting the parks
movement to the dramatic transformation of the United States
brought about by the Civil War. It places California's Yosemite
Valley, the first federally authorized park, in the larger framework of war-related legislative and constitutional reforms that
significantly broadened people's relationship to their national
government and raised their expectations of government's role
improving public life. These momentous changes were contin-
gent on extinguishing slavery and remaking the fatally frac-
tured political system that supported it.

In this context, we examine Olmsted's formative experience working on Central Park against the background of the approaching Civil War. When Central Park was conceived, American cities were growing into diverse, industrialized metropolises with profound environmental and social problems. This challenged the viability of the urban future that Northern states, in particular, had embraced. If cities could not be made more healthful and if their increasingly diverse populations could not be successfully assimilated, urbanization of the nation threatened to be its undoing. It was during the years leading up to the war that Central Park took shape as an embodiment of republican ideals that might bind together the nation during its greatest social and political crisis.

While Central Park was still under construction, Olmsted wrote the "Preliminary Report upon the Yosemite and Big Tree Grove," otherwise known as the "Yosemite Report," described as "one of the most profound and original philosophical statements to emerge from the American conservation movement."[3] Olmsted was called upon to write this report in 1864, after Congress granted Yosemite Valley and the Mariposa Grove—fifteen square miles of granite domes, towering waterfalls, and giant sequoias—to the State of California "for public use, resort, and recreation . . . inalienable for all time."[4] Olmsted used the Yosemite Report not only to apply his park design ideas, honed at Central Park, to the magnificent landscape of Yosemite but also to share his vision for a reconstructed postwar nation where great public parks were keystone institutions of a liberal democracy. He stated in the report that he hoped the country would emerge from four years of bloodshed and social upheaval with renewed dedication to the principles of "equity and benevolence." He believed that the government had a compelling obligation to support great public parks on an equal footing with all other major duties.

In the summer of 1865, Olmsted laid out his ideas in the 7,500-word document (reprinted as part of this volume) affirming a nexus between park making and the advancement of civilization. The concept of national parks implicit in Olmsted's report would begin to gain traction once two significant developments occurred. Congress first had to set aside land taken from the public domain to establish a public reservation. Second, the government had to be prepared to assume responsibility for its permanent protection. In the Yosemite Report, Olmsted carefully chronicled the first development—the passage of the Yosemite Act one year earlier—and presaged the second—the establishment of Yellowstone National Park seven years later.

In a letter to Olmsted in the fall of 1861, Sarah Blake Sturgis Shaw, social reformer and abolitionist, made a remarkably prescient association between emancipation, government reform, and the creation of public parks. Shaw was the mother-in-law of Olmsted's close friend George Curtis and wife of the philanthropist Francis Shaw. When the war broke out, Sarah Shaw collected money and supplies for Union Army medical relief and corresponded with Olmsted in his newly appointed capacity as general secretary of the Sanitary Commission. Shaw's letter, however, concerned more than medical relief. She shared her anxiety about possible European intervention in the war and about the South's "treacherous abominable deceit in preparing so long & with such deeply infamous plotting to secede." She noted that she and some friends had recently visited Central Park, a "lovely place," where "we forgot for a while the war & all its horrors." She complimented Olmsted on his work there, telling him "how fortunate you are to do so much for posterity."[5]

But Sarah Shaw was already looking beyond victory on the battlefield to a future that would justify the terrible war that was unfolding before her eyes. In her letter she framed the conflict as an opportunity to reinvent the nation and replace a political system that had long sanctioned slavery. "If we can re-make the Government, abolish Slavery & get the Central Park well under [way] for our descendants," she wrote Olmsted, "we shall have done a work worthy of the 19th century & ought to be willing to suffer."[6] Her suffering was not rhetorical. Two years later her twenty-five-year-old son, Colonel Robert Gould Shaw, commander of the Fifty-Fourth Massachusetts Regiment, died alongside more than one hundred Black soldiers in an assault on Fort Wagner, on Morris Island, South Carolina.

Shaw's letter was written very early in the war, when putting down the rebellion and reestablishing the Union were paramount objectives for most Northern loyalists. Her choice of words—"re-make the Government"—implied that her goal was not only the restoration of the federal union but its replacement with something better. Her vision was also associated with the creation of a great public park, an achievement representative of the kind of civic progress she wished for the country. These accomplishments were interdependent and together represented for Shaw her highest ambitions for nineteenth-century America. There is no record of Olmsted's reply, but they held the same aspirations. In his 1865 Yosemite Report, Olmsted specifically identified continued work at Central Park—along with construction of the Capitol dome in Washington and the establishment of a public park at Yosemite—as essential projects, in the midst of war, that affirmed the efficacy and value of republican government and the necessity of defending it.

This book is inspired by these words of Sarah Shaw, expressing a conviction shared by Olmsted that park making, abolition, and the reform of government would emerge out of the cauldron of civil war as foundations of a united and improved republic.

ONE

ABOLISHING SLAVERY AND BUILDING CENTRAL PARK

In 1850, Frederick Law Olmsted returned from a walking tour of Britain and parts of Europe with his brother, John Hull Olmsted, and their close friend Charles Loring Brace. At the age of twenty-eight, Olmsted considered himself a scientific farmer. Although he neglected it during his six months of European travel, he owned a farm on the south shore of Staten Island where he employed the latest techniques of fruit tree cultivation and land drainage. But the young farmer was also discovering his literary voice, particularly as he assembled his observations on English landscapes and agricultural practices. In 1852 he published *Walks and Talks of an American Farmer in England*.[1] The book was a moderate success, and Olmsted shifted his career intentions to writing, publishing, and journalism in the literary world of contemporary New York.

The same year his first book was published, Henry J. Raymond, the editor of a new newspaper called the *New-York Daily Times* (the name was changed in 1857 to the *New York Times*), asked Olmsted to travel through the Southern states to provide a firsthand account of the social, agricultural, and human conditions. Olmsted assured Raymond that his reporting would be objective, rather than incendiary or sentimental, and would therefore satisfy Raymond's desire to provide the paper's readers with a candid and factual perspective. With a reference to Harriet Beecher Stowe's popular novel, *Uncle Tom's Cabin*, Olmsted noted that "northern men have, at present, too little information about the South that has not come to them in a very inexact, or in a very suspicious form, as in novels and narratives of fugitive slaves."[2]

For the better part of two years Olmsted traveled across the South from Virginia to Texas writing over forty articles for the *Times* under the byline "Yeoman." His first journey was a four-month tour beginning in early 1852, traveling down the Eastern Seaboard to Savannah, across the Cotton Belt and up through the Mississippi River valley to Memphis. He passed close to Port Royal, which was to figure prominently in his proposed plans for Southern reconstruction drafted nearly a decade later. His dispatches were filled with detailed descriptions of everyone he spoke with and everything he saw. He did not miss much and reported back on it all. On his second journey, a six-month trip started in late 1853, he was accompanied by his brother John. They traveled down the Mississippi River to New Orleans, then west through East Texas to Austin and the Rio Grande. The following year Olmsted began assembling his *Times* reports in what would become a trilogy of books: *A Journey in the Seaboard Slave States* (1856), *A Journey through Texas* (1857), and *A Journey in the Back Country* (1860). In 1861 the books were abridged and edited into a single volume published in Britain as *The Cotton Kingdom*.[3]

Olmsted had not expressed an opinion on slavery early in life. While he was traveling through England, however, he had been constantly challenged on why his country continued to sanction human bondage. He was influenced by that experience and also by his friend and traveling companion, Brace, who was a staunch abolitionist. The same year they made their European trip, the passage of the Fugitive Slave Act forced Olmsted, like so many others, to reassess slavery in the context of their own everyday lives. The enactment of this federal law deeply inflamed public opinion in non-slave states by mandating Northern citizens and their local officials to arrest fugitives, thus becoming complicit in their re-enslavement. Olmsted was so enraged by this law that he threatened to shoot any man who tried to apprehend a fugitive slave that he might choose to shelter.[4]

Olmsted's political outlook would be considered progressive for his time, but he also evinced many prejudices of the era. He identified himself as a "moderate Free-Soiler" and gradualist on the subject of emancipation, rather than as an abolitionist.[5] He was cautious and paternalistic concerning Black suffrage and exercise of political power. Former enslaved people, he believed, had to be properly prepared before being accorded "the free and enlightened exercise of individual independence and responsibility."[6] He detested slavery but struggled to comprehend how people could live decent and dignified lives without being elevated to his own vision of "civilized" behavior. Like most people outside the South, despite his steadfast opposition to slavery's expansion, he was skeptical about interfering with the institution of slavery where it was already well established. In these attitudes he was not out of step with the leaders of the Republican Party (founded in 1854), including Abraham Lincoln.

But as was true for many Americans, Olmsted's thinking on race evolved with time. At the start of his Southern report-

ing, he emphasized the inefficiencies of the slave-based economy of the South rather than its immorality. His first reports
describe the backwardness and improvidence of the South. He
was deeply disturbed by slavery's violence and human degra-
dation; but it was the system's encouragement of wasteful-
ness and disorder that drew his harshest condemnation.[7] The
Southern landscape in his opinion lacked the industriousness
and stewardship of his native New England. Much of what
he witnessed on his Southern travels, including worn-out
and abused countryside, were an affront to his yearning for a
higher level of husbandry, self-improvement, and civilization.
His firsthand observations, however, sharpened his criticism
of slavery. He acknowledged that there was no good reason
to "consider the negro, naturally and essentially, the moral
inferior of the white." In one dispatch back to the *Times* he
declared slavery to be "the greatest sin and shame upon any
nation or people on God's earth."[8]

In a commemorative address, delivered more than a decade
after President Lincoln's death, Frederick Douglass assessed
Lincoln in the context of his times. "Viewed from the genuine
abolition ground," Douglass submitted to his audience, "Mr.
Lincoln seemed tardy, cold, dull, and indifferent; but measur-
ing him by the sentiment of his country, a sentiment he was
bound as a statesman to consult, he was swift, zealous, radical,
and determined."[9] In much the same way it can be said that
Olmsted was condescending, paternalistic, and a self-anointed
polymath on issues of race. However, when measured against
prevailing opinion, he was a daring, fervent, and persistent
adversary of slavery and a steadfast proponent of recognizing
the humanity of Black Americans and their entitlement to fair
treatment.

Olmsted's critical reporting did not go unnoticed in the

South. The April 1854 issue of the *Southern Cultivator* reported on his travels and took particular offense when Olmsted declared it was the duty of "every man in the world to oppose Slavery, to weaken it, to destroy it."[10] The editors explained that Olmsted's current assignment with the *Times* was to report on the South's "Productions, Industry and Resources" in an "impartial manner," noting that "every civility due to a gentleman of character and talent . . . was freely extended to this avowed unprejudiced reporter." They believed that Southern hospitality had been badly repaid. "Now and then a writer achieves an ephemeral reputation by the aid of false pretenses," they asserted, "and the skillful use of high-sounding declamation in behalf of the rights of man, and by denouncing the horrors of slavery."[11]

Olmsted's Southern travel experiences also strengthened his later enthusiasm for Central Park and Yosemite Valley, projects that for him were infused with social purpose. He observed an absence in the South of cultural and civic infrastructure, which he blamed on the region's huge financial investment in slaves. In contrast the North—and especially the New England of his childhood—built public parks, libraries, and schools and demonstrated the beneficial efficacy of these civic institutions. As he made clear a decade later in his 1865 Yosemite Report, the maintenance of such institutions was a singular duty of government. Their paucity in the South divided the nation and threatened the future of a united republic.

Olmsted's Texas experience, in particular, rekindled a passion for republican political movements on both sides of the Atlantic. He befriended German Free-Soil, antislavery settlers in West Texas, including a group of political refugees from the failed European revolutions of 1848. Many of their ideas—such as free higher education, separation of church and state, and opposition to slavery—contrasted sharply with the attitudes of their nativist neighbors.[12] When Olmsted returned from his Texas journey, he raised money to support an émigré newspaper. But the Germans were finding themselves increasingly isolated and harassed by proslavery partisans. Eventually, émigré political organizations and newspapers were suppressed, and many leaders were forced to flee Texas. Despite these setbacks, Olmsted believed that the days of despotic rule around the world were numbered. In a letter to Brace, alluding to the collapsed European revolutions of 1848, he excoriated the anti-republican, autocratic regimes that had crushed these insurrections. He directed his scorn at one European tyrant after another: "Hear it Nicholas! Hear it, Metternich! Hear it Irish landlords! Hear it Scotch lairds and English hunters." He warned the American owners of slaves that their day of reckoning would soon come as well. "Hear it slaveholding sons of America," he declared, "prepare to meet—or avert—your fate."[13]

In 1855, Olmsted left the Staten Island farm in the care of his ailing brother suffering with tuberculosis. He intended to become a professional writer and devote himself full-time to a literary career. While he was getting his books to press, he took a significant step closer to realizing this ambition when he also became a partner in the Dix & Edwards publishing house. Although it would prove a financial failure, the business put Olmsted in contact with many distinguished literary figures of the day, including Washington Irving, Ralph Waldo Emerson, Harriet Beecher Stowe, and Henry Wadsworth Longfellow.

Antislavery politics, however, were never far from his mind. After *A Journey through Texas* was published in 1857, he tried to coax the New England Emigrant Aid Society into financing the establishment of additional Free-Soil settlements in West Texas and beyond, as a bulwark against the further expansion of slavery in the Southwest.[14] He even went so far as to sound out the Cotton Supply Associations of Manchester and Liverpool to see if there were any English workers who might be persuaded to emigrate and join these proposed "free" frontier settlements.[15] In a letter to early conservationist George Perkins Marsh, Olmsted outlined a plan for constricting the growth of Western slavery. "In four years-time a line from Iowa continuously to the Gulf," Olmsted envisaged, "may be occupied with free labor farms." He predicted that slave owning planters "would dare not establish themselves" on lands "too densely settled with energetic free-laborers."[16]

Olmsted continued to stay engaged with the Emigrant Aid Society, which was vigorously supporting Free-Soil settlers in the Kansas Territory fighting off proslavery militia from nearby Missouri. As Kansas became a flashpoint in the ever-widening struggle between proslavery and antislavery partisans, the society raised funds and purchased weapons for their Kansas allies and turned to Olmsted for help. He responded in part by procuring a variety of small arms and a mountain howitzer destined for Kansas.[17] His greatest contribution, however, were words rather than guns. Taking advantage of his growing acquaintance with prominent newspaper editors and publishers, Olmsted persistently promoted the antislavery cause in letters to the editor and editorials inspired, if not actually written, by him. When the *New York Times* ran the editorial "Emigrants and Texas," Olmsted boasted to his father that "the articles on Texas in the Times last week were built of my timber."[18]

While in London on a business trip for Dix & Edwards, Olmsted authored an incisive article for the *Times* expressing his own darkening assessment of America's political situation. He recounted his conversations with several "respected" but unnamed English journalists, former admirers of America who now despaired for the country's future. Slavery in their opinion, wrote Olmsted, was "at the root of all disorder in the United States." They recoiled from reports of proslavery violence in Kansas and disparaged those who carried out "robbery and piracy in order to give strength and stability to an institution in itself barbarous." The Englishmen were shocked by a litany of recent events, particularly the near-fatal caning of Massachusetts senator Charles Sumner on the floor of the U.S. Senate, which they described as "inexpressibly painful and disappointing." "Even your legislators," the journalists asserted, referring to Sumner's assailant, South Carolina congressman Preston Brooks, "are murderers and ruffians." Having lost all faith in the United States, they were compelled to acknowledge "that the experiment of extreme liberalism in America has failed." Finally, offering a hauntingly prescient warning that Americans were "treading over the crust of a volcano," the Englishmen grimly concluded, "history assure[s] us that either a speedy reaction must set in, or that the political system must fall into ruin and dissolution."[19]

With impending ruin and dissolution very much on his mind, Olmsted rededicated himself to the antislavery cause upon his return to New York. Following the publication of *Back Country,* Olmsted intensified his antislavery rhetoric in an introduction and supplement to T. H. Gladstone's *The Englishman in Kansas; Or, Squatter Life and Border Warfare.* In his introduction, Olmsted bitterly condemned Southern complicity in the perpetuation of slavery and all those caught up in exercising the "cruel, inconsiderate, illegal, violent and pitiless" behavior that supported it. Olmsted claimed that these traits were becoming deeply embedded in Southern culture corrupting any claim to "Christian civilization."[20]

Olmsted shifted back and forth between his antislavery agitation and his editorial duties until the financial panic of 1857 bankrupted Dix & Edwards and a subsequent publishing house, Miller & Curtis, with whom he briefly partnered. The financial setback was serious and left him for a time unemployed. And there were further concerns. His brother John, who was his closest friend, traveling companion, and confidante, had left for Europe in January with his wife Mary Cleveland Perkins Olmsted in what would be a futile effort to improve his chronic lung condition. John died that fall in France. Still unmarried, Olmsted had a farm that he had little interest in cultivating and a literary career that, while it brought him some prestige and readership, had not become a basis of financial support. Not for the first or last time, he needed to consider changing the course of his life.

O lmsted retreated to a country inn on the Connecticut shore, nominally to prepare his *Back Country* manuscript for publication. There a fortuitous encounter with Charles Wyllys Elliott, a member of the Central Park Board of Commissioners, resulted in an unexpected opportunity. The board had recently been set up by the state legislature to oversee the creation of an expansive park in New York City. The new board had been established to give the state's Republicans more administrative control over the park's construction and replaced a short-lived municipal park commission dominated by local Democrats. Elliott encouraged Olmsted to apply for the vacant position of superintendent to oversee the work of preparing the site for its development. Wasting no time, Olmsted rushed back to the city to lobby vigorously for the job.

A network of influential friends quickly coalesced to advocate on his behalf. He believed himself to be an ideal candidate given his experience managing farm laborers, his background in scientific agriculture (including tree propagation and drainage technology), his literary skills, and his credibility with the Republican Party, which had a majority of seats on the new park board. Olmsted was appointed to the Central Park position.[21]

Olmsted had already written about important precedents in urban park development, particularly Birkenhead Park near Liverpool, which he had visited in 1850 not long after it opened and which he described enthusiastically in *Walks and Talks*. In 1851, Olmsted met the horticulturist and publisher Andrew Jackson Downing at the landscape gardener's home in the Hudson Valley. There he was introduced to Downing's new partner, the English architect Calvert Vaux, who had recently emigrated to join Downing in his design practice. Downing had been an influential proponent for building a major public park in New York City. His 1851 essay "A Park for New York," along with the persuasive editorials of William Cullen Bryant, galvanized political support for the idea. Tragically, Downing died in a steamboat fire in 1852, but his ideas regarding the benefits and purposes of public parks inspired Olmsted and many others.

Downing maintained that a large new park in New York would become a national symbol of what he called the "refinement of the republic." Such a national symbol of progress was badly needed, he urged, because despite its claimed republican credentials, the country lagged behind Europe in building civilizing institutions such as public libraries, galleries, and parks. "Shame upon our republican compatriots who so little understand the elevating influences of the beautiful in nature and art," Downing wrote, "when enjoyed in the common by thousands and hundreds of thousands of all classes, without distinction!" He argued that a republican nation "in its very idea and tendency" must embrace a "broad program of popular refinement." Downing criticized elites who opposed the park's creation, arguing that they "intrench themselves in . . . *exclusiveness*." These "social doubters," Downing claimed, "mistake our people and their destiny."[22] When Olmsted went to work on Central Park in 1857, he already saw the project as a means of validating and improving republican government in a free society, regardless of the misgivings of "social doubters" in both the North and the South.

Olmsted's role in the creation of Central Park dramatically expanded when the Central Park commissioners organized a design competition for the site, and Calvert Vaux prevailed on Olmsted to collaborate on an entry. Vaux, as the former partner of the revered Downing, was highly qualified for the undertaking. Not only was he a trained architect, he and Downing had produced the most significant public landscape design to date in the United States, their 1851 plan for the Mall in Washington, DC. The reasons Vaux chose to work with Olmsted must be inferred. Certainly Olmsted had some experience—mainly in managing farms—that could be directly useful. More to the point, he also already had an important position as the Central Park construction supervisor and so he clearly had supporters on the board that had recently hired him. His literary and social connections were important, since this would be a great public work requiring skill in its conceptualization, explanation, and presentation as well as its design. Perhaps most important, Olmsted also had acquired over the previous months a great familiarity with the site: its geology, topography, drainage, and existing vegetation. Vaux must have seen the advantage of working with this new partner, and the result, the Greensward

Plan, was a collaborative effort that won the competition and soon proved an enormous success.

Olmsted was promoted to "architect-in-chief" and Vaux was made "consulting architect." During the very years the country was descending into civil war, Central Park took shape through an intensive campaign of construction. Olmsted now administered a huge public works project and, as codesigner with Vaux, continued to develop their schematic competition entry while work was under way in the field. The bones of the landscape—an elaborate system of walks and drives, excavated lakes, massive soil amendments, thousands of planted trees and shrubs—were a priority, since Greensward originally called for few new buildings. The park was opened, largely unfinished, in the winter of 1858, when the newly excavated lake at the center froze over and thousands of ice skaters made use of it. Over the next three years, Olmsted and Vaux completed much of the transformation of 840 acres at what was then the northern edge of the city into what was becoming known as one of the finest urban parks in the world.[23] During the dark war years that followed, work continued, as did the public's use and appreciation of the emerging landscape.

Central Park marked the arrival of a new public institution—the public park—that was rapidly emulated across the country. Urban parks greatly enhanced adjacent real estate values, a fact not lost on municipal officials or speculators, fueling a proliferation of new park commissions. But the new urban landscapes also responded to the social and environmental challenges of nineteenth-century cities, and they embodied a republican ideology associated with the values of social improvement and national unity. Olmsted and Vaux—and increasingly many of their contemporaries in the cities of the Northeast and Upper Midwest—believed that landscapes like

Central Park were essential to public health, social cohesion, the general viability of urban life, and to what they described as a higher level of civilization. "It is one of the great purposes of the Park," explained Olmsted to the Central Park commissioners, "to supply to the hundreds of thousands of tired workers, who have no opportunity to spend their summers in the country, a specimen of God's handiwork that shall be to them, inexpensively, what a month or two in the White Mountains or the Adirondacks is, at great cost, to those in easier circumstances."[24] Central Park provided this refuge and, by doing so, made the city more livable for its inhabitants. The park represented an unprecedented commitment of public resources for a municipal civic project. This was at a time, immediately before the Civil War, when ambitious federal plans for investments in education, transportation, and agriculture were being blocked by proslavery politicians.

By 1858 the national calamity that Olmsted had warned about in his letter to the *Times* two years earlier had only worsened with the Supreme Court's Dred Scott decision. For Olmsted, Central Park represented more than a municipal park project, at a time when the nation, as he had written from England, was "treading over the crust of a volcano." Southern economic and political forces protecting slavery—the "slave power" to abolitionists—seemed ascendant. The South Carolina jurist and U.S. senator William Harper had once claimed that all "great and enduring monuments of human art and industry" were produced by the labor of slaves.[25] Launching an ambitious public project with the intent of elevating all elements of the city's population, built by free—not slave—labor, affirmed republican values at a time when they were most threatened.

The result, Central Park, was a huge popular success

and a national phenomenon. Henry Bellows, an admirer and future employer of Olmsted, described the park in the *Atlantic Monthly* as "the most striking evidence yet of the sovereignty of the people . . . in the history of free institutions,—the best answer yet given to the doubts and fears which have frowned on the theory of self-government."[26] Vaux would refer to the park as "the big art work of the Republic."[27] Olmsted would later point out that the completion of Central Park in the midst of the Civil War was a defiant symbol of the durability and promise of the United States when the country's future as a unified nation was seriously threatened by secession and armed insurrection. He saw the park as an expression of democratic achievement and another reason to defend the Union. "It is of great importance as the first real park made in this country," he wrote, and was "a democratic development of the highest importance."[28]

The popularity of Central Park changed Olmsted's life. By 1859 the park was becoming famous and, to a lesser degree, so was he. In that year he also married Mary, the widow of his brother John, and at the age of thirty-seven he became stepfather to their three young children. The impending war would bring further change. As busy as his life had become, Olmsted maintained his antislavery activism, finally publishing *A Journey in the Back Country* in 1860. By the time his fourth book came out, people on both sides of the Mason-Dixon Line were already anticipating war. Any interest in better understanding the workings of Southern society was now superseded by a preoccupation with looming disunion. Olmsted considered secession a form of anarchy and called for the "dogma of state rights" to be "annihilated."[29] Even steadfast abolitionists now shifted their attention from the issue of slavery to secession, viewed as a dagger aimed at the heart of popular democracy.

When Abraham Lincoln was elected in November 1860, South Carolina and several other states declared their intention to reject the election's outcome and secede by the year's end. Federal property within these states, including forts and arsenals, were either occupied by Southern state militias or threatened with seizure. During "Secession Winter," seven Southern states, followed by four more after hostilities began at Fort Sumter, formed the Confederate States of America. As the crisis unfolded, Olmsted did not intend to sit on the sidelines. In December 1860 he wrote his friend Brace, "my mind is made up for a fight. The sooner we get used to it the better."[30] To his father he wrote, "I consider it a religious duty to strengthen the government by any means in my power."[31]

His London publisher urged Olmsted to produce a condensed compilation of his previous books on the South. The resulting volume, *The Cotton Kingdom*, was directed to an English audience in the hope that it would help deter support for the Confederacy. Before the war, South Carolina senator James Hammond had infamously declared that the absolute economic power of cotton "could bring the whole world to our feet."[32] Playing off Hammond's rhetoric, Olmsted hoped that his book might sway public opinion and convince the British government not to buy Southern cotton or offer material support to the rebellion. Olmsted took time from his duties at Central Park to rush the book to press.

As a companion to *The Cotton Kingdom*, Olmsted created an unusual map illustrating an inverse relationship between overall cotton productivity and the density of the South's slave population. He drew from his experiences in the South, where he observed that free labor was often more productive than slave labor. He hoped the map would help convince cotton-dependent England that supporting or intervening on behalf of the Confederacy would not be in their long-term economic interest. Olmsted's cotton map was remarkably similar to another map, prepared about the same time by the United States Coast Survey under the direction of Alexander Bache.[33] The "Map Showing the Distribution of the Slave Population of the Southern States of the United States" used statistical cartography to display the geographic distribution of enslaved people in every county in the South—much like Olmsted's cotton map. In the upcoming war, Bache's map would be used strategically by the Lincoln administration to recruit freed people into the ranks of the Union Army and disrupt the South's slave economy.[34] The similarities between Olmsted's and Bache's maps were not likely accidental, as the two men knew each other, and both served with the U.S. Sanitary Commission.

In spring 1861, as hostilities began, Olmsted searched for a role in the war effort. A carriage accident in Central Park in 1860 had left him seriously lame, and so active military duty was precluded. He believed that his Southern travels and reporting qualified him to oversee "the elevation and improvement of the negro" and to direct the transition of newly liberated people to productive lives as free men and women.[35] He hoped that once such potential for improvement was demonstrated to white Southerners, they would eventually come to recognize that slavery was an impediment to their "honor, safety and economic prosperity." This misplaced confidence in the latent loyalty and reasonableness of Southern whites was shared by many Northerners, including President Lincoln for a time. Olmsted held onto this conviction in spite of having once quoted in his book *A Journey in the Seaboard Slave States* an editorial from a Richmond newspaper that unequivocally stated: "It is all a hallucination to suppose that we are ever going to get rid of African Slavery, or that it will ever be desirable to do so. It is a thing that we cannot do without, that is righteous, profitable, and permanent, and that belongs to Southern society as inherently, intricately, and durably as the white race itself."[36]

In June 1861, only weeks after the first refugees fleeing enslavement sought sanctuary at Fort Monroe, in Virginia, Olmsted offered his services to the government as a national commissioner of contrabands to direct "the proper management of negroes in a state of limbo between slavery & freedom." He asserted that he had worked out "practically every solution of the slavery question—long ago advocated in my book," and that the assignment was "really something I am pining to find, in this war."[37] He was not taken up on his offer.

As an alternative, Olmsted accepted a senior position with the Sanitary Commission, a privately run medical relief organization chartered by President Lincoln. As soon as the war began, it became increasingly evident that prolonged combat would involve military casualties which would outstrip the capacity of the undersized and underprepared army medical bureau. The commission's president, the Unitarian minister and civic leader Henry Bellows, looking for a general secretary to administer the commission, set his sights on Olmsted, whom he had recently praised for his work on Central Park. Olmsted's success as a public works administrator made him a good choice to organize the unprecedented relief effort. When offered the position, Olmsted chose not to cut his ties with Central Park but instead took a leave of absence.

For the better part of two years Olmsted devoted himself to strengthening Union medical services. He initially focused on sanitation. "The duty of guarding against the defeat of our armies by disease," he wrote, "needs to be undertaken as earnestly, as vigilantly, . . . with as resolute a determination, as any other military duty." Lest he be accused of being "over-zealous," Olmsted defended his rhetoric. "In the life-struggle of a nation," he declared, "soft speaking of real dangers and over-considerateness is a crime."[38] He involved himself in a number of important innovations, including the establishment of an extensive network of supply depots directly behind Union lines. In early 1862, during the ill-fated Peninsula campaign, he applied this concept more broadly to include field hospitals by creating a flotilla of hospital ships that would closely follow the army's movements. It was in reference to this bloody and terrible campaign that Olmsted described a "republic of suffering."[39]

Olmsted pushed himself mentally and physically to the point of exhaustion. Though he passionately believed in his work, he was greatly distressed by what he perceived as slights by the military hierarchy and rivals within his own organization. He possessed a brilliant capacity for planning, organization, and attention to detail; he could also be demanding and unyielding. Bellows, Olmsted's steadfast champion, praised his "integrity & talent for organization, patriotism and genius." Katharine Prescott Wormeley, who worked directly under Olmsted in the field, commended him as a man "of the most resolute self-will, —generally a very wise will," who ran an organization where "no inefficiency was tolerated, where the work was thoroughly and conscientiously done." Wormeley added, however, that she thought Olmsted was born with autocratic tendencies— though she was quick to add that as an autocrat he was "very satisfactory to be under."[40] The diarist George Templeton Strong, a Sanitary Commission board member, praised Olmsted as the "most remarkable specimen of human nature with whom I have ever been brought into close relations. . . . Talent and energy most rare." But Strong also complained about Olmsted's "monomania for system and organization on paper . . .

and appetite for power. . . . Were he not among the truest, purest, and best of men we should be in irreconcilable conflict."[41]

Even after joining the Sanitary Commission, Olmsted held out hope that an appointment working with freedpeople might still be possible. In 1862 he thought his chance had finally come when he offered his services to the "Port Royal Experiment." Populated almost entirely by former slaves, Port Royal, South Carolina, and adjacent areas along the Southeast coast had been occupied by Union forces in the fall of 1861 to establish supply bases for the U.S. Navy's blockading fleet. A program was begun, initially supervised by the Treasury Department, to educate and employ these freedpeople in an early model for reconstruction. With the help of Northern philanthropists, the Port Royal Experiment, as it was called, provided education and medical care for liberated Black Sea Island communities and organized a program of contract labor on plantations abandoned by their owners. Several Northerners such as the abolitionist Lydia Maria Child suggested a leadership role for Olmsted, praising his antislavery credentials, "agricultural knowledge," and "enlightened views about labor."[42]

Accompanied by Sanitary Commission board members Henry Bellows and Alexander Bache, Olmsted personally lobbied Treasury secretary Salmon Chase for the job of running the Port Royal program, and having devised his own plan for Port Royal, Olmsted worked behind the scenes on advancing legislation in Congress. He wrote to President Lincoln with advice on training and educating Port Royal freedpeople "in a few simple, essential and fundamental social duties of free men in civilized life."[43] There is no record of a reply. In a letter to a congressman about Port Royal, Olmsted criticized "controlling minds in Washington" for their "listlessness, indifference and utter childish cowardice."[44] His outspokenness once again likely got in the way of his ambition; a military officer was put in charge of the Port Royal Experiment.

Like many antislavery Republicans, Olmsted was skeptical of the Lincoln administration's competence and early caution on emancipation, once referring to "our imbecile government" in a letter to his wife.[45] He described Lincoln himself more favorably as "amiable, honest," but felt at the time that the president had "no tact, not a spark of genius."[46] His opinion of Lincoln grew markedly more favorable when the preliminary Emancipation Proclamation was issued in September 1862.

Early in 1863, Olmsted, Wolcott Gibbs, and other Sanitary Commission associates organized the Union League Club in New York to mobilize political support for a broader set of war objectives. Olmsted and Gibbs envisioned an organization with a strong educational mission dedicated to the Union cause and promoting emancipation. Members of the New York club were drawn mainly from the ranks of Republican business and civic elites, but Olmsted saw an opportunity for creating a national organization with a broader appeal. Writing to Gibbs, he suggested that clubs should be "extended over the whole country" to advance education and social reform.[47] And they were. Union Leagues formed in Boston and Philadelphia and in smaller cities and towns across the Northern states. Olmsted, however, quickly became disillusioned with the direction of the movement, believing that the leagues had abandoned their original purpose of reform and instead primarily dedicated themselves to promoting national loyalty and the war effort. As the conflict wound down, so did the Northern Union Leagues, except for a handful that were transformed into elite social clubs that exist to this day. After the war, new Union League organizations were founded across the South to support Republican-led Reconstruction and Black rights. Recruiting many African

American war veterans, these Southern leagues pursued a broader social agenda as originally envisioned by Olmsted and Gibbs, engaging in community organizing, voter registration, and self-defense.[48]

All the while Olmsted continued to keep his hand in Central Park affairs, retaining the title of superintendent and, when he was able, overseeing maintenance projects and new planting. In April 1862 he and Vaux were jointly appointed by the park commissioners as consulting architects for Central Park. This appointment was made despite Olmsted's largely being absent due to his wartime responsibilities, and it fell primarily to Vaux to revise the plan for the upper area of the park. Olmsted still held out hope that one day he would return to Central Park as full-time superintendent "in fact as well as name."[49]

In the fall of 1862 a serious schism began to develop within the ranks of the Sanitary Commission, when local branches began asserting more control over funding and medical activities. Olmsted believed that such "localism" siphoned off critical resources into parallel and less-efficient operations. This led to a bitter, drawn-out tug-of-war over the distribution of private contributions. The situation reached a critical point at the time of the battle of Antietam, in September 1862. Battlefield casualties at Antietam were staggering, stretching the commission's resources to the breaking point. In desperation, Olmsted looked west to California for help.

As the war raged on and Olmsted and Vaux forged ahead with their Central Park work, in far-off California interest in a very different landscape was stirring. Yosemite Valley was becoming known as the greatest scenic wonder of the West. The valley's nearly eight miles of perpendicular granite walls and the nearby Mariposa Grove of giant sequoias, with five hundred mammoth trees nearly three hundred feet high and almost sixty feet in circumference, beggared belief. Yosemite, despite the claims of its promoters, was not a wilderness. The area had been used by Indigenous peoples for thousands of years before non-native immigrants, about the time of the 1849 Gold Rush, invaded the Yosemite region and violently expelled the inhabitants. When California became a state in 1850, aboriginal land claims were unilaterally extinguished as these lands, including Yosemite Valley and the Mariposa Grove, were incorporated into the public domain and opened for homesteading.

By the late 1850s a steady stream of publicists and entrepreneurs began to promote Yosemite and the Mariposa Grove as a destination for adventuresome visitors including artists, photographers, and a number of dignitaries. Among them was Horace Greeley, the influential editor of the *New York Tribune,* who made the long journey to Yosemite in 1859. Greeley declared after his visit, "I know no single wonder of nature on earth which can claim a superiority over the Yosemite."[50] Yosemite was soon to have a new champion. In April 1860 the transplanted New England minister Thomas Starr King arrived in San Francisco. A protégé of Henry Bellows, he came to lead the city's growing Unitarian congregation. King had written a popular book about New Hampshire's scenic White Mountains, and he immediately took a keen interest in Yosemite Valley and the Sierras.[51] In the late spring, soon after settling his family into their new San Francisco home, he joined a few like-minded parishioners on an expedition to Yosemite. Along the way they stopped at the sprawling Mariposa mining estate situated in the Sierra foothills not far from their destination. The estate was run by its major shareholder, John C. Frémont, a former explorer, soldier, and Republican presidential candidate. At first glance it would seem that Frémont, the heroic "pathfinder" of the West, would have little in common with King, the freethinking clergyman from the East. Both Frémont and King, however, were particularly outspoken in their opposition to slavery and support for the Union at a time when the threat of secession was hanging over the country and California's political leanings appeared uncertain.[52]

King's journey to Yosemite Valley and the Mariposa Grove inspired him to write a series of eight articles for the *Boston Evening Transcript,* titled "A Vacation among the Sierras: Yosemite in 1860." King was overawed by the scale of everything he saw. He tried to compare Yosemite's features to his beloved White Mountains. Of "the sublime rock called 'El Capitan' or the Chieftain," he reported: "This wonderful piece of natural masonry stands at an angle with the valley. . . . And how high, think you? 3,817 feet! . . . Remember, too, that it stands straight. There is no easy curve line as in the sides of the White Mountain Notch. . . . A more majestic object than this rock I expect never to see on this planet. Great is granite, and the Yo-Semite is its prophet!"[53]

Back in San Francisco, King was drawn into a small circle of acquaintances often convened by Jessie Benton Frémont at her Black Point home on the edge of San Francisco Bay. Many of those who gravitated around Jessie Frémont, the "pathfinder's" charismatic wife, were familiar with Yosemite Valley. They included King, the photographer Carleton Watkins, writer and poet Bret Harte, and attorney Frederick Billings. Watkins was a young photographer who would make a national name for himself with his stunning photographic portfolio of Yosemite Valley and the giant sequoias of the Mariposa Grove. Billings, a self-made man of many dimensions, was a business partner of John Frémont; both were investors in the Mariposa Estate that King had visited. It was through the Mariposa property that Billings would later make Olmsted's acquaintance. Billings may also have been involved in advancing the idea for the Yosemite Grant, and later, as an officer of the Northern Pacific Railroad, he promoted Yellowstone National Park as well.

Billings shared King's enthusiasm for the spectacular landscape of Yosemite, but it was their mutual commitment to the Republican Party and the Union that would have the most immediate consequences as the crisis over slavery and secession came to a head in the fall of 1860. Jesse Frémont recruited King, an eloquent and increasingly popular orator, to give a series of public speeches urging Californians to stand with the republic and reject secession. King delivered a series of impassioned speeches around the state drawing unusually large pro-Union audiences in California's principal cities at a critical moment when legislators in Sacramento were paying close attention. Describing his fiery oration to a friend, King recalled, "I pitched into secession. . . . I pledged California . . . to a flag that should have no treacherous threads of cotton in its warp."[54] Frémont boasted to King that had he lived in California longer she would have made him a United States senator.[55]

King's efforts won him friends and admirers on both sides of the continent, binding California more closely to the Union and the Republican Party and helping set the stage for the state's ascending national role. Ralph Waldo Emerson would exuberantly write King asserting that "the salvation and future of California are mainly in your hands."[56] King's fellow Unitarian minister S. P. Dewey wrote to him praising the loyalty of California: "tempted as she has been with prospects of sovereign power which she need only have stretched out her hand to take, she is the truest of the true."[57]

As the war progressed, King turned his talents to fund-raising for the Sanitary Commission. Just as the beleaguered agency's national office was on the verge of insolvency in September 1862, California, with King's leadership, came through with the first of several cash infusions that enabled the commission to function through the end of the war. Bellows, in a telegram to King, affirmed that "California has been our main support in money, if she fails us we are lost."[58] Bellows was not exaggerating; as the single largest financial contributor to the Sanitary Commission, California donated over $1.2 million for the care of wounded Union soldiers, one-quarter of all funds raised nationwide and four times the amount raised by the second-largest donor state, New York.[59] Despite his substantial investment of time and energy on behalf of the Union, King's ardor for Yosemite never flagged. His zeal for the land permeated his ministry; in a sermon titled "Lessons from the Sierra Nevada," he urged his parishioners to create "majestic landscapes for the heart," and "Yosemites in the soul."[60]

Though California's support helped ease the Sanitary Commission's financial crisis, the fractious organization's internal struggles intensified. By the summer of 1863, following the battle of Gettysburg, an exhausted Olmsted, feeling undercut and undervalued, decided he had had enough and resigned his position with the agency. He had hoped that his services, based on his considerable knowledge of the South—"five years of hard study I gave to the practical difficulties of Slavery"—and his obvious administrative experience, would be recognized and sought out by the Lincoln administration as it began to plan for postwar reconstruction. In a moment of self-reflection, however, Olmsted realized that such a summons would not be forthcoming. He complained to Bellows that his books and "practical suggestions" were better known and carried more

influence with the British Parliament than with his own government. Despite a "general chance of usefulness in the settlement
of war questions," he confided in a letter to Mary, "I am in
danger of estimating too highly the value of my judgement."[61]
Olmsted, still stung by his Port Royal rejection, likely realized
that he had burned too many bridges.

Once again at a turning point in his life, an opportunity
appeared unexpectedly. Frémont's Mariposa mining operation in Bear Valley had been sold to new investors who were
seeking a manager, and Olmsted, concerned about supporting
his growing family, expressed interest. He believed his talents
could be applied in California's frontier environment with "a
much more certain . . . prospect of exercising a powerful &
within certain limits controlling influence."[62] Vaux urged him
to remain East, later writing, "you are off at the other end of
the world, depriving the public of your proper services."[63] With
the war still raging, Bellows appealed to Olmsted's patriotism,
declaring, "the country cannot spare you at such a junction."[64]
Olmsted was not swayed and decided to accept the Mariposa
position. Little did Vaux or Bellows realize that, in California,
Olmsted would soon enough be back in his country's service
and once again be making a mark in the history of American
parks.

Arriving in San Francisco in the fall of 1863, Olmsted
remained in close contact with Bellows and still conducted some
Sanitary Commission business. He arranged to meet Thomas
Starr King; though the two were not personally acquainted,
they had been collaborating at a distance for more than a year.
Olmsted gave King a letter from Bellows thanking him for his
fundraising and emphasizing "the necessity of California's continuing generous support of the San. Commission."[65] Olmsted
and King met on a number of occasions to discuss commission

affairs. Considering their mutual interests, it is likely that the conversation also touched on Yosemite, especially given King's enthusiasm for the wonders of the Sierra and Olmsted's connection with Central Park. In fact, a month after their first meeting, Olmsted went to see the Mariposa Grove for himself.

When Olmsted assumed his new responsibilities, he discovered little about the Mariposa mining enterprise that impressed him. When Frederick Billings gave him a tour of the operation, Olmsted was stunned by how far the estate's facilities had deteriorated under Frémont's earlier management. He was further distressed to learn that mine production had been exaggerated and was, in fact, declining. He would say of Frémont, "Here at Mariposa I stand in his shoes and am paying his debts."[66] Olmsted's administration of the mine was plagued from the beginning by ownership disputes and opaque financial dealings. His New York employers largely ignored his frequent appeals for guidance and help to resolve financial and governance issues. The whole enterprise was hobbled by labor unrest and the threat of insolvency, as angry creditors attached liens on the estate, siphoning off assets badly needed to maintain productivity. Olmsted nevertheless applied himself with typical intensity to his work, demonstrating his aptitude for efficient administration and managing to keep the mine in operation for a further two years.

His time was better spent, however, on other projects in California of much greater consequence. His initial discomfort with the semiarid landscape soon developed into understanding, appreciation, and finally new approaches to landscape design adapted to Western climates and soils. As it became clear that Mariposa would not be a long-term employer, Olmsted responded to requests for his services as a landscape designer. During these years, in fact, he designed his first complete park system, for San Francisco in 1864. Though it was unexecuted, the plan demonstrated an innovative approach to designing public landscapes for Western cities, one that made sense in semiarid climates. He also produced plans for what would become the University of California Berkeley campus (also unimplemented) and other commissions. His California experience would later prove invaluable when he was called on to design the Stanford University campus in the 1880s.[67]

Olmsted's most significant opportunity in California came in 1864 when a bill to protect Yosemite Valley was introduced in Congress. With Olmsted and King in California at the time, it would seem logical that the Yosemite legislation might have originated in some way with them. This was not the case; but neither was their presence entirely inconsequential. Earlier that year, King, only thirty-nine, died suddenly from diphtheria and pneumonia, likely brought on by his nonstop work. Twenty thousand people gathered for his funeral, and the California legislature adjourned for three days in his honor. By order of President Lincoln, minute guns were fired from the coastal forts ringing San Francisco Bay.[68] "San Francisco has lost one of her chief attractions," editorialized the *San Francisco Bulletin,* "the state, its noblest orator; the country, one of her ablest defenders."[69]

What would be the most significant acknowledgment of King's legacy began several weeks before his death when California's Republican senator John Conness started work on drafting legislation that would grant Yosemite Valley and the nearby Mariposa Grove of giant sequoias to the State of California to be made into a public park. Israel Ward Raymond, a representative of the Central American Steamship Transit Company of New York, had written Conness recommending that the thirty-eight thousand acres be permanently withdrawn from the public domain and closed to all future settlement claims and that a park be created to protect these lands from private exploitation.[70] By accepting the federal grant California would agree to manage the acreage "for public use, resort, and recreation . . . inalienable for all time." These were Raymond's words, and when Conness forwarded Raymond's letter to the General Land Office with a request to draft a bill, he insisted this specific language be included. Raymond's letter also recommended that California create a commission to prepare a plan for the new park and suggested a number of individuals to serve on it. Olmsted's name was at the top of the list.

Raymond's motivations must be inferred. But access to Yosemite for visitors at the time involved taking his company's steamships upriver to the docks at Stockton and from there proceeding by road. An increase in tourism would be a direct corporate benefit. While neither Olmsted nor King may have had direct contact with Raymond, King's untimely death and Olmsted's presence at the nearby Mariposa Estate likely influenced Raymond and suggested how Yosemite could become a public park. In any case, the legislation's backers agreed that Olmsted would be the most qualified person to recommend how that transition should take place. Conness introduced his bill for the Yosemite Grant on March 28, 1864.

TWO

REMAKING GOVERNMENT AND
THE YOSEMITE GRANT

B y the mid-nineteenth century, the federal government already had a long history of making large grants of lands to new states, for the purposes of building roads and canals and as a reward to military veterans. The government's largest asset was land, especially its vast holdings in the West. Almost everywhere, the sovereignty of Indigenous occupants was violated or simply ignored often in flagrant violation of treaty obligations. Native resistance was brutally crushed in a long series of military campaigns that expelled Indigenous populations and expropriated their lands. Incorporated into the "public domain," much of this land was sold to finance the operation of the federal government, pay off its debts, and encourage westward expansion and settlement. In the 1850s, the emergent Republican Party began to look beyond the sale of public land and turned to federal land grants as a mechanism for enacting several of the party's national policy priorities. One of these was building a transcontinental railroad that would bind California closer to the Union. Another was establishing a national system of public colleges that would advance agriculture and industry and create a more educated electorate.

Southern Democrats in Congress mobilized to block these Republican-sponsored land-grant bills, which they feared would work against the long-term interests of slave owners in multiple ways.[1] They favored a relatively weak central government that they could control. Since the country's founding, slave interests had exercised a disproportionate influence on the functioning of all three branches of government and sought to limit the size and duties of the state by choking off potential sources of revenue. They opposed direct taxation, particularly of slave property, and resisted tariffs that primarily benefited Northern manufacturers.[2] There was much at stake. In 1860, 20 percent of the nation's wealth was invested in the ownership of slaves—more than the combined value of all factories and railroads in the country.[3] Sixty percent of all exports, principally cotton, was produced by slave labor. Democrats feared that a stronger, more active central government, with access to greater resources, would enact improvements that would primarily benefit non-slaveholders, mainly Free-Soil farmers and settlers, natural constituents of a growing Republican Party committed to the containment of slavery. They therefore opposed the land grants and did what they could to limit the small federal government to narrowly defined objectives—overseeing foreign relations, collecting customs revenues, maintaining military posts, delivering the mail, and apprehending fugitive slaves.

Republican-proposed land-grant college legislation would enable states to build and endow public colleges and universities accessible to people of modest means.[4] Public higher education would promote economic innovation and improve agricultural practices. In the words of the bill's chief sponsor, Vermont congressman Justin Morrill, the new colleges would not only encourage the "rejuvenation of worn-out lands," but they would also help small farmers moving west.[5] Southern slave owners and their Democratic allies feared that the political and economic power of the slave states would be diminished by the inverse improvement in the lives and opportunities of people in free states and territories. Their preferred remedy to potential depletion of existing plantation lands in the Cotton Belt was to encourage expansion of slavery in Western territories, leading to more territories eventually entering the union as slave states.

When Morrill introduced the legislation in 1859, Senator Clement Clay of Alabama, leading the Democratic opposition, denounced the bill as "one of the most monstrous, iniquitous and dangerous measures which have ever been submitted to Congress." "If the people demand the patronage of the federal government for agriculture and education," Clay declared, "it is because they have been debauched and led astray."[6] In the House of Representatives, Alabama congressman Williamson Cobb warned that a dangerous precedent was being set. "If the policy is embarked in," he asked, "what shall be its limits?" The national government, according to Cobb, might one day be moved to "feed the hungry and clothe the naked" and build and support "common schools."[7] Cobb believed that public lands should generate revenue in lieu of taxes and not be used for social purposes.[8] Senator Jefferson Davis of Mississippi argued that if the bill was approved the government would be "warped so far from the path it had previously followed."[9] Investment in public education was not a priority in the South, as Olmsted had observed in his "Letter to a Southern Friend"; in fact, it was feared as a destabilizing influence on slavery.[10] Virginia senator James Mason made this explicit during the debate. "Would it not be in the power of a majority in Congress," he asked, "to fasten upon the southern States that peculiar system of free schools in the New England States, which I believe would tend . . . to destroy that peculiar character which

I am happy to believe belongs to the great mass of the southern people."[11] Despite this opposition, a coalition of Republicans and a few Northern Democrats managed to narrowly pass the Land-Grant College bill. It was promptly vetoed by President James Buchanan, a Northern Democrat anxious to appease the Southern wing of his party.

Southern Democrats also derailed homestead land-grant legislation, which Buchanan vetoed a year after the college bill. The homestead bill proposed that any citizen or immigrant could gain title to 160 acres of public land if they cultivated it for five years. Southern lawmakers saw the homesteaders in direct competition with Western slave owners seeking large tracts of land for expansion of slavery in the territories. Furthermore, they feared that grants for homesteading would stimulate Free-Soil settlement, inevitably leading to more free states, tipping the balance of power in Washington. Not surprisingly, their attacks on the homestead bill echoed their denunciations of the land-grant college legislation. "We look upon the bill as one of the worst and most fatal achievements of abolitionism—," the *Weekly Georgia Telegraph* editorialized; "it will amount in the end to supporting Northern pauperism out of the National Treasury." The *Telegraph* described Northern life as "all . . . strife and antagonism," while in the South, the editors maintained, "all is harmony—servants never so valuable—never so well cared for—never more contented and happy; masters never so prosperous."[12]

Following the election of 1860, the balance of power in Congress was upended with the secession of eleven states. As senators and congressmen, all Democrats, from the seceding Southern states withdrew from the new Thirty-Seventh Congress, the Republican Party gained large majorities in both chambers. James Buchanan retired to his country estate in

Pennsylvania, his veto pen set aside forever. His successor, Republican Abraham Lincoln, prepared to lead the country not only to save the Union but also in the enactment of a national legislative agenda that could only be achieved with the legislative majority his party now commanded. In his first annual message to Congress in December 1861, Lincoln declared that he was "anxious and careful" that the war "not degenerate into a violent and remorseless revolutionary struggle." But in his second annual message a year later, he acknowledged that the situation demanded profound changes. "The dogmas of the quiet past are inadequate to the stormy present," he warned, "and we must rise with the occasion. As our case is new, so we must think anew and act anew. We must disenthrall ourselves, and then we shall save our country."[13]

The events of the war hastened the new reality that Lincoln predicted. Barely a month after the attack on Fort Sumter, General Benjamin Butler, commander of the Union garrison at Fort Monroe on the coast of Virginia, refused to return escaped slaves employed by nearby rebel forces. Congress sanctioned Butler's initiative with passage of the First Confiscation Act in August 1861, allowing the seizure and holding of property, including enslaved people used by rebels for "insurrectionary purposes." The Federal occupation of Port Royal and adjacent Sea Islands, established to support the Union naval blockade, accelerated the flight of Black refugees from inland plantations to the perceived freedom and safety of Union lines.

These coastal enclaves became densely populated with formerly enslaved people. As further coastal incursions deep in Confederate territory were carried out in support of the blockade, Olmsted clearly recognized the social, political, and military implications.[14] In a detailed letter to the *New York Times* in December 1861, he advised that "if Government should take possession of certain districts of the South . . . and should offer at all of these a safe harbor for all negroes, there can be no doubt that slave property throughout the South would become rapidly less controllable than it is at present and as rapidly less valuable." He further explained how the new Confiscation Act could be applied in tandem with current and future military actions by taking advantage of the data visualized in the maps he and Bache had drawn up. "Negroes in the rebel states are property," he wrote, "and as property, are the very sinews of the rebellion. . . . whenever our forces penetrate the rebel States, it is in our power to sever these sinews." African Americans who fled to the Union lines not only denied the Confederate economy the service of their labor, but their example encouraged the further destabilization of slavery throughout the interior South. "A hostile force would thus invade the enemy in his very stronghold . . . ," Olmsted pointed out, "with every negro who ran away and escaped immediate pursuit, the tendency to disregard control among those remaining would increase in strength." He also called for the fugitives to be "safely and humanely cared for" by the government, a standard that the Union Army, which oversaw swelling contraband camps, failed to meet.[15]

By the spring of 1862, Union forces had seized New Orleans, the South's largest commercial port, and occupied much of the Mississippi River valley. What this meant, based on Olmsted's and Bache's maps, was that Union forces, operating far from main battlefields, had moved into regions with the densest concentrations of enslaved people in the entire South, just as Olmsted had advised. Federal advances into the Mississippi Delta, according to historian James Oakes, "brought more than 150,000 slaves into Union lines. These numbers . . . put a great deal of pressure on Union emancipation policy."[16] The exact status of hundreds of thousands of contraband refugees was ambiguous, but it was now impossible to imagine these people ever being returned to slavery.

Hope for a quick Union victory or a negotiated settlement with the rebellious states faded after a year of escalating civil war. A sobering realization set in as casualties mounted: there would be no return to the antebellum status quo. "I would rather go through the farce of acknowledging Southern independence," Olmsted remarked in a letter, "than have the Union ever again as it was."[17]

Early that spring, a war-hardened president and Congress, encouraged by military successes along the Southern coast and in the Mississippi Valley, were ready to advance a sweeping Republican legislative agenda that had been delayed by the outbreak of war. A war that was begun on the premise of "saving the union" was evolving inexorably into the "violent and remorseless revolutionary struggle" that Lincoln had once hoped to avoid. This Republican agenda expanded the purposes of the war, enacting a vision of a "more perfect union" that eventually extended to a far-reaching national program of emancipation—what the historians David Blight and James McPherson described as "our second revolution."[18] The war represented, in Blight's words, "the destruction and death of that first American Republic and the invention and beginning of the second Republic." The withdrawal of Southern legislators from Congress removed a roadblock that had long held Republican initiatives in check. The eleven Southern states that left the Union no longer stood in the way of a Republican Party that believed, according to Blight, in "energetic, interventionist government" and was prepared to become "an agent of change . . . of the economy and . . . the maximization of human equality."[19] Lincoln and his congressional allies were ready to intervene on a continental scale, on behalf of emancipation and free labor, agrarian opportunity, national improvements, and public education.

Over a period of five months, from March to July 1862, Lincoln and the Thirty-Seventh Congress got to work. They started with measures targeting slavery, including an article of war prohibiting army officers from returning fugitive slaves, outlawing slavery in the District of Columbia, and a total ban on slavery in all territories of the United States. This put an end to the long series of territorial compromises over slavery going back to the Northwest Ordinance of 1787. Along with the passage of reintroduced homestead legislation, a new Department of Agriculture was established to provide statistical and technical information aiding farmers. As the summer wore on, congressional momentum increased.

On July 1, 1862, Lincoln signed the Pacific Railway Act, authorizing and subsidizing (mainly through land grants) the construction of a transcontinental railroad binding California ever closer to the republic. The railroad would tie the West to the East even as the North was still divided from the South. On the following day, Lincoln signed the long-delayed Land-Grant College Act, setting aside fifteen million acres of land to underwrite new agricultural colleges across the country. On July 17, the president signed the Second Confiscation Act. The First Confiscation Act had declared enslaved persons pressed into war-related labor by the Confederacy as seized "contraband" of war, transforming Federal outposts in the South such as Fort Monroe and Port Royal into safe havens for a growing tide of refugees. The Second Confiscation Act freed every enslaved person in areas occupied by Union forces.

Lincoln and his generals knew that every action that weakened slavery diminished the Confederacy's capacity to fight. To this end, the first steps were taken to recruit Black soldiers into the Union Army. On the same day the president signed the Second Confiscation Act, Congress also passed the Militia Act, authorizing the use of African Americans for military service. Freedom was guaranteed to all those who served and their families if they had been previously enslaved by rebels. "We have reached a point in this great war," declared one Republican congressman, "when we should employ them on our side, and grant them freedom as a boon for faithful assistance, if they are willing to render it."[20]

Olmsted placed great faith in the fighting ability of formerly enslaved Black men. "As to the capacity of the negro to be a soldier, I have no doubt," he testified before the government's American Freedmen's Inquiry Commission, "I have myself seen them manifest every quality asked for in a soldier. I believe many of them are capable of making military heroes." Olmsted also recommended to the commissioners that Black soldiers should be treated with respect. He understood that in the ranks of the Union Army they would likely encounter prejudice, inferior treatment, petty humiliations, and unique dangers. "If the government arms & equips them as it does white soldiers," Olmsted predicted, "pays them as it does white soldiers," freedmen would fight well.[21]

Concerns about the treatment of Black soldiers, placed in segregated regiments commanded by white officers, were well founded. They were initially paid a third less than white troops. In fact, the government fell short on every one of Olmsted's recommendations. It was not until June 1864, after sustained protest, that Congress stipulated that Black troops should receive the same uniforms, equipment, and pay as white soldiers. Olmsted also called attention to the protection of Black combatants should they become prisoners of war. Jefferson Davis pledged to re-enslave captured African American soldiers and execute their white officers. Given atrocities like Fort Pillow, where surrendering Black troops were executed, Lincoln had to respond. He issued an Order of Retaliation threatening Confederate prisoners with hard labor or worse if Black prisoners were harmed, explaining, "It is the duty of every government to give protection to its citizens, of whatever class, color, or condition, and especially to those who are duly organized as soldiers in the public service."

Lincoln had long understood that the nation could not stand "half slave and half free," and that the existential threat slavery posed to the precepts of American democracy had led, perhaps inevitably, to a slaveholders' rebellion bent on the destruction of the nation. Up until the summer of 1862 the president had proceeded cautiously on slavery. Not wishing to alienate border state loyalists or get too far out in front of the general electorate, Lincoln floated various schemes for gradual compensated emancipation and even colonization. But other realities confronted him, at home and abroad. The war's outcome hinged to a large extent on the diplomatic front in Europe. If England or France recognized the Confederacy—or used their navies to break the U.S. blockade of rebel ports—the Union cause might not recover. "We are losing the confidence and sympathy of our best friends in Europe," warned George Perkins Marsh, Lincoln's envoy to the newly established Italian republic. According to Marsh, the United States had lost popular support "because irresolution, timidity and tergiversation of our government . . . have given rise to grave doubts as to its honesty of purpose and especially as to its sincerity in respect to the slave question."[22] As a consequence, Union advocates sought to influence opinion in Europe and assert the righteousness of their cause. Publication of Olmsted's *Cotton Kingdom* in England had been one such effort.

At home, Union military incursions into the South, continued to motivate slave resistance including the exodus of nearly half a million people fleeing enslavement and their deepening collaboration with advancing Federal forces. Perceiving that the government was now on their side, former slaves and even those still enslaved provided critical aid to Union allies by scouting, gathering military intelligence, providing succor to escaped Federal prisoners, laboring for the army, and eventually fighting as Union soldiers. As Olmsted had correctly predicted, every blow against slavery was a blow against the rebellion. The irreversible consequences of this movement of African American self-liberation and intensifying collaboration with the Union Army highlighted the need to elevate the war's objectives and, in Lincoln's own words, "act anew."

On September 22, 1862, President Lincoln, using war powers, issued a preliminary Emancipation Proclamation, the capstone of five of the most transformative months in the history of the United States. The proclamation stated that as of January 1863, "all persons held as slaves within any State, or designated part of a State, the people whereof shall then be in rebellion against the United States shall be then, thenceforward, and forever free." A total end of slavery would not be codified in the Constitution until the Thirteenth Amendment was adopted in 1865, but Lincoln had made clear which direction the country was now headed. "In giving freedom to the slave," he declared, "we assure freedom to the free," indelibly linking emancipation with every other achievement of Congress and his administration.[23]

Though white supremacist Northern Democrats were fiercely critical of the proclamation, Republican discontent with Lincoln receded. Antislavery proponents, such as Olmsted and King, rallied to the president and cheered his recasting of the war's larger meaning. Olmsted wasted no time in praising Lincoln's move with great passion, declaring, "Slavery and republican liberty cannot exist together." After the final Emancipation Proclamation was signed, he avowed, "I shall stand by it . . . as long as I live."[24] The Emancipation Proclamation swiftly led to the recruitment and arming of thousands of Black troops, most former slaves. Frederick Douglass assessed the inevitable political outcome: "Once let the black man get upon his person the brass letter, U.S.," Douglass predicted, "let him get an eagle on his button, and a musket on his shoulder and bullets in his pocket, there is no power on earth that can deny that he has earned the right to citizenship."[25]

The proclamation not only damaged the Confederacy's war-making capacity, but just as important, it gave the conflict that larger meaning so many abroad had sought. "The danger of recognition, or of the encouragement of recognition, in England," wrote Olmsted in 1863, "has been completely removed. . . . It was not before the Proclamation."[26] Together with all the other components of Republican reform, the proclamation represented a promise of reinvigorated American freedom that clarified why the war, despite the enormous personal sacrifices being asked, was worth continuing to fight. A Union officer, Colonel Régis de Trobriand, wrote, "The time for disguise had passed"; the conflict had "at last assumed its true character." Looking to the future, Trobriand declared, "It was no longer a question of the Union *as it was* . . . ; it was the Union *as it should be*."[27]

The struggle to make "the Union as it should be" would continue throughout the war and include sweeping social, political, and economic changes. A national banking and revenue system, public education, public works, and the settlement and development of public lands all figured in the larger program of remaking government. The Civil War was, as Lincoln said, "a People's contest," and government existed to help the people.[28] "Improvement in its various forms," noted the historian Mark Fiege, "became the means by which he prosecuted the war and preserved the Union."[29] These reforms also changed people's relationship with the nation. The new income tax, for example, connected every taxpayer directly, for the first time, with the federal government.[30] The federal mobilization of resources and manpower was unprecedented; entirely new governmental bureaus were established. Before the war began in 1861, there were fewer than six thousand federal workers. By the end of the war, the government's Quartermaster Corps alone was employing more than one hundred thousand people. The Bureau of Refugees, Freedmen, and Abandoned Lands, temporarily established in response to the refugee crisis in the South, became the nation's first social welfare agency. The department, known as the Freedmen's Bureau, did things the national government had never tried to do before: setting up schools, reuniting families, overseeing labor contracts, and organizing the redistribution of confiscated and abandoned lands. Many of these efforts were short-lived or drastically scaled back in postwar years, but the government had demonstrated unprecedented resiliency and capacity. Congress would later act based on these precedents.

Land grants proved a pivotal mechanism for advancing this broader agenda of wartime Republican legislative reform. In the spring of 1864, a relatively modest land-grant bill was introduced in Congress to protect California's Yosemite Valley as a public reservation in the spirit of Central Park. There was little debate. The Lincoln administration was beholden to Thomas Starr King and other influential friends of Yosemite, including Olmsted, for their steadfast allegiance to the Union, support of emancipation, and financial contributions to the war effort. This accumulated political capital created a favorable environment for the Yosemite proposal in Washington. The difficult reelection campaign Lincoln was facing in fall 1864, for which he needed the support of California's Republicans, was another compelling reason to endorse the Yosemite legislation.[31]

Similar to the Land-Grant College and Homestead Acts that preceded it, the Yosemite Act achieved a desired civic improvement by the granting of public land. Olmsted later explained the Yosemite Grant as more than a land grant to a state, or as Senator Conness had awkwardly described it, a legislative accommodation for "various gentlemen in California."[32] Olmsted more accurately labeled the grant "a trust from the whole nation," explicitly preserving Yosemite for all the people of the United States. The California state geologist and future Yosemite commissioner, Josiah Whitney, emphasized the singularity of the transfer. "This was not an ordinary gift of land," Whitney pointed out, "to be sold and the proceeds used as desired; but a trust imposed on the State, of the nature of a solemn compact, forever binding after having been once accepted."[33] If California had declined to accept the trust, the reservation would have remained with the federal government. Less than two months after the bill was introduced, it was passed by Congress and was signed into law by President Lincoln on June 30, 1864.[34]

Many historians who have written about the Yosemite Grant have failed to recognize the context of the act as a wartime measure. Some categorized the grant as an inexplicable anomaly, a departure from established public land policy by distracted lawmakers and having nothing at all to do with the war. To the contrary, the Yosemite Grant was a direct consequence of the war and related to the political and social revolution that the conflict fueled. The grant was not an anomaly but an embodiment of the ongoing process of remaking government. Nor was the measure passed by an inattentive Congress distracted by wartime crises. The late spring and early summer of 1864 were indeed a perilous time for the United Sates as it entered the fourth year of civil war. Military offensives in Virginia and Georgia had incurred staggering battlefield losses. Lincoln's confidence in his own chances in the coming fall elections was badly shaken. But Congress's action on Yosemite can be interpreted as an intentional assertion of a steadfast belief in the eventual Union victory and an acknowledgment of the political debt owed to California loyalists, including the recently deceased King. Like other pieces of reform legislation moving through Congress, the Yosemite bill affirmed the government's capacity to function and entertain new ideas and initiatives even while operating under great duress. The Yosemite Grant can also be seen as another small component of the government's public land policy in the American West—one of a series of legislative actions that included the Homestead, Land-Grant College, and Pacific Railway Acts. For obvious reasons, Republicans in Congress had long supported legislation that would strengthen ties with Western states and territories and promote national unity.[35]

These policies facilitated the westward migration during the war of nearly one million new settlers. For those who had recently emigrated to America or desired a fresh start, these policies were welcome. But Indigenous people were never included among the beneficiaries of this "new birth of freedom." In Yosemite Valley and across the United States, tribes were forced out of ancestral lands repurposed to expedite Republican land policies that the Lincoln administration championed. The creation of parks such as Yosemite came at the expense of Native people's exile and suffering. Early writers who described Yosemite Valley as untrammeled wild nature willfully overlooked generations of human occupation. Despite expressions of humanitarian concern for Indians found in Olmsted's writings, for him, like other nineteenth-century conservationists, Native Americans remained largely invisible. As time went on, Indigenous tribes across the West would endure further displacement and dispossession tied to other landscape preservation efforts.

The intended beneficiaries of land grants, mostly white farming families whose husbands and sons were fighting for the Union in large numbers, were given new opportunities consistent with overall Republican efforts to redefine and expand rewards of American citizenship. These rewards were closely identified with Union victory, explicitly repudiating the antebellum American republic that assiduously protected the economic interests of a small slaveholding elite. Lincoln advanced a new, expansive vision of a republic based on emancipation and the establishment of a government "of the people, by the people, and for the people." When the Department of Agriculture was established in 1862, he declared that the new agency had been created "for the more immediate benefit of a large class of our most valuable citizens."[36] Lincoln and the Republicans offered a deal that the historian Ari Kelman described as "fight for Lincoln and later for liberty, and as fair recompense for . . . patriotic sacrifices receive an education, access to expertise, and land connected by transportation to markets."[37] There were other strong incentives to embrace this deal. Voting for Lincoln and, however reluctantly, for emancipation, introduced Black troops onto the battlefield to help shoulder the burden of fighting and hasten the day the rebellion would be put down and the war would be won.

The government's reservation of Yosemite's spectacular landscape for "public use, resort and recreation" was another part of this bargain. It was a modest but consequential component of a much broader program of national improvements that together with the ending of slavery was at the core of the Republican argument for fighting on to victory.

Olmsted first entered Yosemite Valley in August 1864, after the Yosemite Act had been signed. He was overwhelmed, as he wrote in the Yosemite Report: "This union of the deepest sublimity with the deepest beauty of nature, not in one feature or another, not in one part or one scene or another, not any landscape that can be framed by itself, but all around and wherever the visitor goes, constitutes the Yo Semite the greatest glory of nature." He did not see Yosemite Valley as John Muir did, as an imagined and sanctified wilderness. Olmsted understood it in aesthetic terms and found a unique and powerful composition of landscape effects, or scenes. Intimate and picturesque scenery could be found along the winding Merced River. Around the river the valley opened up into expanses of pastoral meadows. While camping in the valley with his family, he wrote to his father back in Connecticut that "the valley is as sweet & peaceful as the meadows of the Avon."[38] And everywhere the pastoral expanse of wet meadows was set directly against the awesome and sublime heights of the granite walls. It was the compositions of perfectly juxtaposed types of scenery and landscape experience that made Yosemite, for Olmsted, "the noblest park or pleasure ground in the world."

Upon returning to Bear Valley from Yosemite in the fall, Olmsted learned that he had been appointed by California's governor Frederick Low to head the new commission established by the state in accordance with the terms of the federal land grant.[39] Charged with the management of the grant, the Yosemite commissioners, under Olmsted's guidance, were to prepare recommendations for how the valley should become a park. Olmsted was selected as commission chair most likely based on his reputation as an administrator. At the age of forty-two, he was a respected Unionist, known for his wartime leadership of the U.S. Sanitary Commission. But it was his experience designing and supervising the development of Central Park that gave him unique qualifications for the position.

Just as the wartime political origins of the Yosemite Grant have been obscured over the years, so have the connections between the new parks in New York City and Yosemite Valley. But the two projects shared more than contemporary Republican ideology: they were both conceived as public parks in the 1860s at a time when that institution was first taking shape in the United States. Olmsted, Vaux, and other early landscape architects were responsible for devising how the places selected to become parks would be physically developed—and (especially in Olmsted's case) invested with symbolism and meaning in the context of a remade republic. Olmsted wrote the Yosemite Report between September 1864 and August 1865. The report has many dimensions and purposes and includes far more than his specific recommendations for the development of the Yosemite Valley landscape to facilitate its protection and enjoyment. Those design suggestions are found in the last few pages of the report. But Olmsted's plan nevertheless reveals the ways in which the country's prototypical American urban park and its first national reservation shared essential origins in the practice of landscape design and in the meaning and social utility invested in American parks across scales and contexts.

Olmsted envisioned Yosemite Valley as a public landscape that would eventually be visited by millions of people a year, just as Central Park already was. If their geographic settings differed entirely, their effective size did not. The area of Yosemite Valley in which most visitors would congregate (the valley floor) was not much more than 1,500 acres, while Central Park covered 840 acres. And for Olmsted, the essential purpose of both parks—and therefore the intent of any design intervention—was consistent: assuring that the experience of landscape beauty was preserved, enhanced, and made accessible to all, not just to a privileged few. His task as a landscape designer, in both cases, was to plan an approach to development that would allow the public to have those experiences without destroying what they had come to enjoy in the process. In urban parks, landscape scenes often had to be improved and engineered to achieve the desired effects. Pastoral expanses needed to be graded and planted into existence; lakes had to be excavated and filled; soils required amendments and subsurface drainage; trees and shrubs had to be planted by the thousands to frame and create views and spaces. But this was above all, as Olmsted practiced it, an art of composition: the creation of a sequence of "larger landscape effects," or scenes, that provided a range of experiences of the natural world through a framework of landscape aesthetics.

He explained exactly what this meant in 1866, in his report for Brooklyn's Prospect Park commissioners. An existing park site, however propitious, was unlikely to exhibit a series of "ideal" landscape types, or experiences and was even less likely to possess them "harmoniously related to one another." But it was clear that through careful study of the site, its inherent "ideals" could be developed, or improved, and brought together in a unified composition, creating a considered sequence of, for example, pastoral and picturesque landscape scenes. "The result would be a work of art," he and Vaux wrote, and the production of such "landscape compositions . . . we denominate landscape architecture."[40]

No landscape composition could survive, however, if paths, drives, and other features did not channel visitor traffic and prevent an unregulated flow of humanity from trampling it into dust. Circulation systems, therefore, would not only choreograph the public's movement and assure a full experience of the composed effects but would also prevent the damage that millions of feet, not to mention vehicles, were otherwise bound to have. And there was another vital function of the elaborate and overlaid systems of paths, bridle paths, and carriage drives Olmsted and Vaux created in New York and Brooklyn in the 1860s. They observed that urban parks had two somewhat antagonistic purposes. The first was to make "scenery offering the most agreeable contrast to the rest of the town" freely available to all. The second was the "opportunity for people to come together for the single purpose of enjoyment, unembarrassed by the limitations with which they are surrounded at home."[41] If the first was necessary to individual health and well-being, it was threatened by the second, equally important, purpose, to provide public spaces for diverse and large congregations of the public.

People coming together in parks enhanced a sense of community and an affirmation of common values and identity. Without this kind of public use, parks might be beautiful landscape compositions, but they would have no social utility or larger meaning. Cities such as New York had grown through unprecedented immigration that threatened and often manifested in sectarian and ethnic strife. The republic itself was suffering through its greatest and most violent episode of disunion.

The rhetoric and the ideal of people coming together in diverse and large groups in the setting of landscape parks appealed as a vision of social cohesion. And thousands of people at a time could come together in large groups—and also benefit from the soothing and healthful experiences of park scenery—through the careful design of circulation and gathering spaces coordinated within the larger landscape composition. The landscape design could preserve the individual experience of natural beauty by accommodating gatherings or activities at strategic points. The right design would maintain the integrity of the experience—and of the landscape—for everyone.

Olmsted's design suggestions for the Yosemite Valley landscape should be seen in this context: as his assessment of the inherent potential of the site as a composition of landscape scenes, leading to his judgment of what needed to be done to make that composition available to the public while preventing its destruction and assuring that even large numbers of people could experience it fully. This was park making—landscape architecture—as Olmsted was defining it. At Yosemite the composition of landscape scenes already existed. The valley could become "the noblest park or pleasure-ground in the world" because it was already a unique juxtaposition of "sublime" granite walls and the "beautiful" valley floor. The "first point to be kept in mind," therefore, was "the preservation and maintenance as exactly as is possible of the natural scenery," which required "the restriction . . . within the narrowest limits consistent with the necessary accommodation of visitors, of all artificial constructions and the prevention of all constructions markedly inharmonious with the scenery." Olmsted knew that "an injury to the scenery so slight that it may be unheeded by any visitor now, will be one of deplorable magnitude" when multiplied by millions.

Some of the formal features of urban park design, specifically drives and paths, were readily adaptable to the Yosemite Valley landscape and served the same ultimate purposes. Olmsted suggested the construction of a one-way carriage loop (up one side of the valley and down the other) "which shall enable visitors to make a complete circuit . . . reaching all the finer points of view . . . with suitable resting spots and turnouts . . . at frequent intervals." Such a drive would reduce the "necessity for artificial construction within the narrowest possible limits." The circuit drive would be complemented by a system of pedestrian paths leading to "points of view accessible only by foot." Other suggestions addressed the specific needs of the new type of park Yosemite was to become. Five cabins near "convenient camping places" would be occupied by tenants charged with maintaining "one comfortable room as a free resting place for visitors and the proper private accommodations for women," as well as supplying "simple necessities for camping parties."

There were direct precedents for Olmsted's approach at Yosemite expressed in the 1858 Greensward Plan for Central Park. That report began with the suggested treatment of the north end of the park, which was farthest from the city (still concentrated well to the south of the park at the time) and which retained some forest cover over a rocky terrain. Noting that the wooded and picturesque character of the still-remote north end "already was the highest ideal that [could] be aimed at for a park under any circumstances," Olmsted and Vaux suggested that it be "interfered with . . . as little as possible." Their plan called for the continuation of the park drive through the area and for pedestrian paths and overlooks; but otherwise no formal planting, buildings, or anything else should detract from the "ideal" character that already existed. They emphasized that throughout the park "architectural structures should be confessedly subservient to the main idea," that the experience of landscapes "should always be uppermost in the mind of the beholder." As Olmsted did at Yosemite seven years later, they anticipated that the number of visitors would increase dramatically as the city grew, which they provided for with features such as drives and paths that would maximize enjoyment and minimize impact.

Olmsted and Vaux asserted that experiencing landscape beauty was the principal benefit Central Park could offer, and so it should not be compromised by the erection of large buildings or the siting of otherwise worthy institutions that would undermine the institution of the park, as they were defining it.[42] Yosemite Valley was an extension and continuation of that institution—the American public park—to a regional scale. The geographical context was entirely new, but the design approach as well as the purposes and ideological justifications remained constant. Whether on Manhattan Island or in the Sierra Nevada, the challenge of park design was to protect the landscape—whether "improved" or left as undisturbed as possible—from unintentional damage while enhancing the public's experience. For Olmsted there was no inherent contradiction—as long as the park was managed through the minimal interventions he described, a successful design could achieve both objectives. The largest item in his proposed budget, in fact, was for improving the road from the valley to the steamboat docks at Stockton, which would make the trip more affordable for larger numbers of people. The road would also make it possible to ship in supplies, avoiding the necessity of converting the valley's natural meadows into hay fields, pastures, orchards, and farms to provide for the public.

In the twentieth century, historians and officials obscured the links between municipal and national parks, favoring separate origins and inventors of a "national park idea." But Central Park and Yosemite Valley were both products of the practice of park making that Olmsted, Vaux, and others were pioneering. Both epitomized the new institution of the public park in the United States. Both embodied the midcentury Republican ideology of improvement, progress, and union so important before, during, and after the Civil War. The public figures involved in popularizing Yosemite in California, such as King, Greeley, Billings, Watkins, and Olmsted, were from the East and at the very least knew Central Park well and approved of everything it represented. Circumstances placed Olmsted in California just at the moment that the future management of Yosemite was being seriously considered. He was the right person in the right place at the right time to address the new park's larger meaning and context in relation to the outcome of the war and the country's future.

Olmsted seized the opportunity to address much more than design suggestions for the new park, using the Yosemite Report to place before the American people his particular vision for parks in postwar America at a pivotal moment in the nation's history. The historian and former National Park Service director Roger Kennedy marveled at the report's "breadth of comprehension," which could "unite discussion of the statue of Liberty atop the Capitol dome, the emancipation of the slaves, the destruction of the earth of the South by the plantation system, the prospect of equally disastrous destruction of the Yosemite Valley and the giant sequoias, public education through the Morrill Act, and homestead legislation."[43] The Yosemite Report established the basic scaffolding for further development of the American park movement and an emerging idea for national parks. The report affirmed for the first time every citizen's entitlement to enjoy the nation's most spectacular landscapes—and the responsibility of government to make it possible.

Olmsted began by placing the project squarely in the context of the still-ongoing national struggle: "It was during one of the darkest hours, before Sherman had begun the march upon Atlanta," he wrote, "or Grant his terrible movement through the Wilderness," that Congress had realized the value of Yosemite to the nation and "consideration was first given to the danger that such scenes might become private property." He compared the federal grant of Yosemite to other great works of civic art that had continued through the war years, including Central Park and the Capitol dome in Washington. Both were highly symbolic statements about the future of a reunified nation. Solomon Foot of Vermont declared on the floor of the Senate, "We are strong enough to, thank God, to put down this rebellion and to put up this our capitol at the same time."[44] President Lincoln is reported to have said, "If the people see the capitol going on, it is a sign we intend the Union shall go on."[45] Olmsted pointed to the continuing work on the Capitol as emblematic of national renewal—taking place within view of rebel soldiers positioned across the Potomac River. "The great dome of the Capitol was wholly constructed during the war," he wrote in introducing his report, "and the forces of the insurgents watched it rounding upward to completion for nearly a year before they were forced from their entrenchments on the opposite bank." The establishment of Yosemite as a public park was another civic accomplishment of a reunifying nation.

The political ideology of American parks, as Olmsted presented it, was complex and had international ramifications. The transition of Yosemite Valley into a public park demonstrated the strength and benefits of a republican form of government at a time when republican movements in Europe were struggling against autocratic regimes. The editors of the *New York Times* chastised "dynastic and aristocratic Europe" for offering sympathy and covert support for the Confederacy. They described America's ongoing conflict as a "war in favor of a privileged class; a war upon the working classes; a war against popular majorities; a war to establish in the New World the very principles which underlie every throne of Europe." A Confederate victory would prove America's "democratic experiment a failure."[46] The global implications of a Union victory were clearly on Lincoln's mind at Gettysburg when he declared, "Now we are engaged in a great civil war, testing whether that nation, or any nation so conceived and so dedicated, can long endure."[47]

Olmsted was also acutely aware of this international contest between popular, republican government and anti-democratic, oligarchical rule, and he made that contest central to his emerging park philosophy. He cited many examples of aristocratic privilege monopolizing natural resources and recreational opportunities. "Men who are rich enough and who are sufficiently free from anxiety with regard to their wealth," he wrote in the report, "can and do provide places of this needed recreation for themselves. They have done so from the earliest periods known in the history of the world, for the great men of the Babylonians, the Persians and the Hebrews, had their rural retreats, as large and as luxurious as those of the aristocracy of Europe at present." Even in Britain, which he was greatly attached to, "there are . . . more than one thousand private parks and notable grounds devoted to luxury and recreation," available only to the aristocracy and wealthy classes. "The enjoyment of the choicest natural scenes in the country and the means of recreation connected with them," he warned, "is thus a monopoly . . . of a very few, very rich people. The great mass of society, including those to whom it would be of the greatest benefit, is excluded from it," consigned by old world governing classes to "spend their lives in almost constant labor."

In contrast, access and enjoyment of landscape beauty and nature would be a right of citizenship rather than a prerogative of great wealth in a reconstructed American republic. This right aligned with Republican policies that upheld a role for government in helping to level the playing field, guaranteeing all Americans access to resources and education. Lincoln described the war as "a struggle for maintaining in the world that form and substance of government whose leading object is to elevate the condition of men; to lift artificial weights from all shoulders; to clear the paths of laudable pursuit for all; to afford all an unfettered start and a fair chance in the race of life."[48] Olmsted, as Lincoln did, evoked the language of the Declaration of Independence to frame his argument that guaranteeing "pursuit of happiness against all the obstacles" was an obligation of the republic. He looked forward to a government, powerful enough and righteous enough, to overcome such obstacles "otherwise insurmountable, which the selfishness of individuals or combinations of individuals is liable to interpose to that pursuit."

Olmsted also placed the Yosemite Grant in the cultural context of midcentury American art that had for decades been rooted in varied responses to the nation's landscapes. He knew how significant contemporary painting, photography, and literature were to his own approach to landscape design and to the broader public parks constituency that he was cultivating. Olmsted recounts in the report that during the years leading up to the Yosemite Grant, "a livelier susceptibility to the influence of art was apparent, and greater progress in the manifestations of artistic talent was made, than in any similar period before in the history of the country." He was likely referring at least in part to the great metropolitan Sanitary Fairs that were held in major cities across the North to raise funds for the Sanitary Commission and other war relief organizations. Exhibitions of art were the centerpieces of these events and brought in needed revenue. The fair art galleries also served to raise morale, rekindle patriotic feelings, and according to one scholar provide "visual proof of the magnificence of the American land and the character of its people."[49] Albert Bierstadt's *Valley of the Yosemite,* one of 360 paintings displayed at New York's Metropolitan Sanitary Fair in April 1864, commanded the highest price for any piece of art sold at this elaborate eighteen-day public event.[50]

Olmsted specifically credited the influence of the photographer Carleton Watkins and the painter Albert Bierstadt, both well known to him and Thomas Starr King, for nurturing the nation's "susceptibility to the influence of art" and building support for Yosemite's protection. Watkins's presentation albums of his stunning large-format plates and stereo views of Yosemite were sent to key people and institutions in the East, including New York's Goupil Gallery, where the images were exhibited in 1862. The eastern distribution of Watkins's Yosemite portfolios required a considerable investment of time and money. Advocates for the preservation of Yosemite, including Raymond, Billings, and King, likely paid for multiple sets and used their connections to place them in influential hands. King, who knew Watkins through Jesse Frémont's Black Point circle, sent portfolios to Oliver Wendell Holmes and Ralph Waldo Emerson. Frederick Billings, another member of the circle, sent a portfolio to Louis Agassiz and kept a set for himself.[51] William Brewer of the California Geological Survey, on behalf of Josiah Whitney, sent photographs to Benjamin Silliman Jr., professor of chemistry at Yale, and the celebrated botanist Asa

Gray. Israel Ward Raymond included a number of Watkins photographs with his letter to Senator Conness.[52]

Albert Bierstadt, who saw the Goupil exhibition, later painted Yosemite Valley on a trip west in 1863, sponsored by the Union Pacific Railroad and sanctioned by the War Department. Before the last leg of his trip to Yosemite Valley, Bierstadt dined at King's San Francisco home, where he closely studied a portfolio of Watkins's photographs and left behind as a parting gift a sketch of King's daughter.[53] Upon first seeing Yosemite, Bierstadt wrote his friend John Hay, Lincoln's private secretary, "We are now here in the garden of Eden I call it. The most magnificent place I was ever in."[54] Bierstadt went on to create numerous canvases of the valley in his New York studio, based on sketches he made while in Yosemite. The paintings, which were highly lucrative for him, helped establish Yosemite in the public's imagination.

It was when "the paintings of Bierstadt and the photographs of Watkins, both productions of the War time, had given to the people on the Atlantic some idea of the sublimity of the Yo Semite, and of the stateliness of the neighboring Sequoia grove," wrote Olmsted in his report, "that consideration was first given to the danger that such scenes might become private property and through . . . caprice or the requirements of some industrial speculation . . . their value to posterity be injured." In response to the threat that the public might lose access to the "sublimity of the Yo Semite," Olmsted reported, Congress had passed "an act providing that the premises should be segregated from the general domain of the public lands, and devoted forever to popular resort and recreation." For the first time, he emphasized, Congress had preserved in perpetuity a site of particularly outstanding natural scenery, deciding to "treat it differently from other parts of the public domain." Once this step had been

taken, the national government's assumption of a more direct
stewardship role became more likely, if not inevitable.

Olmsted highlighted the revolutionary nature of this act,
reminding his readers that a decade earlier such a national
awakening appeared very far off. Olmsted included in the
report a passage from Downing's 1851 essay "A Park for New
York."[55] For Downing, as for Olmsted, education and culture represented the "true sunshine of the soul." In making a
case for Central Park, Downing had repudiated the cynicism
of opponents to such great public undertakings, whom he
denounced for having "no faith in the refinement of a republic." Downing had anticipated it might take decades, perhaps
not until the next century, for a truly republican spirit to take
hold in America. He could not have imagined the immediate
success of Central Park and how quickly the country would be
transformed by the traumatic events of the Civil War. Before
leaving for California, when Union victory was appearing more
assured, Olmsted wrote, "Thank God we live so close upon
it." He predicted that it was only a matter of time before the
Southern slaveholders' republic and the world's largest system
of human bondage on which it was based were overthrown. It
was, he declared, "more than I had expected a hundred years
would bring the world to."[56] Olmsted contended in the Yosemite
Report that Downing's hoped-for "refinement" of the republic
was taking place. In the context of this great national transformation, the completion of Central Park and the creation of a
park at Yosemite provided further proof that the influence of
education and culture were being elevated to an unprecedented
level in the country's affairs.

The most significant assertions Olmsted made in the
Yosemite Report, however, suggested the necessity as well as
the desirability of the park movement in which the Yosemite

Grant was such an important milestone. He stated that it was "a scientific fact that the occasional contemplation of natural scenes of an impressive character" was "favorable to the health and vigor of men . . . beyond any other conditions that can be offered them." This firm belief in the regenerative powers of nature in undoing a broad array of social harms had guided Olmsted since he began his work at Central Park. Given the importance of accessibility to places such as Yosemite in fostering and supporting public happiness, the future "establishment by government of great public grounds for the free enjoyment of the people" was "justified and enforced as a political duty." All Americans, Olmsted believed, should have an opportunity to lead healthy and fulfilled lives. Removing obstacles to achieving this fundamental goal was "the main duty of government, if it is not the sole duty of government." In this regard the United States could set an example. "Seldom if ever before," he noted, "has proper respect been paid by any government" to this sovereign responsibility. The United States should demonstrate to the nations of the world how an enlightened republic fulfills its duties to its citizens.

As Olmsted had pointed out, in the Old World the natural desire of the affluent was to monopolize great scenic places. This should not be allowed to happen in the United States. It was a responsibility of government "to withhold . . . from the grasp of individuals, all places favorable in scenery to the recreation of the mind and body." Olmsted was clearly writing about the federal government, not California or any other state or political entity. With no available mechanism immediately at hand to protect Yosemite and the Mariposa Grove, Congress had made the expedient decision to entrust Yosemite Valley to the care of California, and the grant had been readily accepted by the state. The Yosemite Commission was submitting its report and recommendations for park expenditures to the legislature and governor of California, but in Olmsted's view, this was a formality, given that the park represented "the will of the nation as embodied in the act of Congress." Yosemite Valley and Mariposa Grove would forever remain a "trust from the whole nation," and as such, the national interest had been established in perpetuity.[57]

Olmsted was also keenly interested in looking at the larger context of Yosemite, beyond the particular circumstances of the grant itself, establishing Congress's responsibility for the protection of future parks in other scenic areas of America. A war was just concluding which reaffirmed the legitimacy of national sovereignty. The federal government was becoming the guarantor of individual rights that had previously been the responsibility of state governments to interpret and protect as they saw fit. Among those rights, asserted Olmsted, was the right of unfettered access to the scenery of great landscapes such as Yosemite. He made clear that it was the duty of the national government, not a local or state government, to ensure that the "enjoyment of the choicest natural scenes in the country and the means of recreation associated with them" be "laid open to the use of the body of the people." This was a uniquely federal charge, comparable in many ways to the nation's responsibility for maintaining military installations. "Like certain defensive points upon our coast," he contended in the report, Yosemite Valley "shall be held solely for public purposes." Here was the intellectual foundation for building a national park system.

Olmsted was not alone in recognizing the opportunities presented by Union victory. Others assumed as well that the country was on the cusp of great social progress from which there would be no retreat. Frederick Douglass, whom Olmsted admired, experienced, albeit briefly, the same burst of postwar optimism. Douglass envisioned an "emancipated and progressive Republic" that he hoped would continue to "frame measures to meet the demands of constantly increasing expansion of power, responsibility and duty." Douglass declared, "The storm has been weathered, and portents are nearly all in our favor. . . . If our action shall be in accordance with the principles of justice, liberty, and perfect human equality, no eloquence can adequately portray the greatness and grandeur of the future of the Republic."[58] A new publication, *The Nation,* also believed that the battle for equity and benevolent government had largely been won and that the country's embrace of republican values was now irreversible. "It is not simply the triumph of American democracy that we rejoice over," wrote the editors in the magazine's inaugural issue, "but the triumph of democratic principles everywhere, for this is involved in the successful issue of our struggle with the rebellion. . . . We utter no idle boast, when we say that if the conflict of the ages, the great strife between the few and the many, between privilege and equality, between law and power, between opinion and the sword, was not closed on the day on which Lee threw down his arms, the issue was placed beyond doubt."[59]

Sharing interests very similar to Olmsted's, George Perkins Marsh hoped for an enlightened period of great environmental reform, now that the war had been won.[60] Marsh wrote in his book *Man and Nature,* published in 1864, that he distrusted the concentration of knowledge in the hands of experts and elites and that he believed all men could be "co-workers with nature" to improve their landscapes and livelihoods. His vision for public land stewardship, like Olmsted's vision for great public grounds, was built on similar republican principles. Marsh considered it "a great misfortune to the American Union" for governments to have "so generally disposed of their original

domain to private citizens." Like Olmsted, Marsh argued for
the designation of large public reservations of land to be set
aside for education and recreation. "It is desirable that some
large and easily accessible region of American soil should
remain, as far as possible, in its primitive condition," he wrote,
"at once a museum for the instruction of the student, a garden
for the recreation of the lover of nature, and an asylum where
indigenous tree, and humble plant that loves the shade, and fish
and fowl and four-footed beast, may dwell and perpetuate their
kind."[61] Both Olmsted and Marsh had worked tirelessly for
eventual Union victory, and with the end of the conflict, both
believed that in postwar America the wind was now at their
back and their ideas for the nation's future would be embraced.

In early 1865, with the Mariposa mining operation rapidly
going downhill, Olmsted relocated to San Francisco to facilitate communication with the mine's New York owners. It was
increasingly clear that his time with the Mariposa Estate was
coming to an end. He remained in San Francisco throughout
the late spring and early summer months and used the time
to complete the Yosemite Report. During his stay there, the
Civil War finally came to an end, and Olmsted joined the
city's jubilant celebration of Lee's surrender at Appomattox.
Only five days later, he shared the enormous display of grief
over Lincoln's assassination. In a letter to Frederick Newman
Knapp, his Sanitary Commission colleague and friend, Olmsted described a public gathering at Thomas Starr King's former church to mourn Lincoln's death, where "every man and
woman in the house was shedding tears. Indeed I never saw
anything that compared at all with the public feeling." Olmsted

did not escape the somber mood. He worried about Lincoln's successor, Andrew Johnson. "Mr. Lincoln is dead, and we have got a man for President whom I don't like," he wrote Knapp, " . . . an essentially uncivilized man, a man of prejudice & bad temper, a very dangerous man." Despite these misgivings, in his letter to Knapp, Olmsted tried to assess the current moment in the best possible light. Reminiscent of the confidence shown by Sarah Shaw in her letter to him four years earlier, when she wrote of remaking government, abolishing slavery, and completing Central Park, Olmsted wrote with tempered optimism, "At any rate, the nation lives and is immortal and Slavery is dead. Enough for us."[62]

During his sojourn in San Francisco, Olmsted was also able to work on a number of landscape projects around the Bay Area, including his plan for the campus of California's new land-grant college in Berkeley and his unexecuted proposal for a park system for San Francisco. These projects, secured in part with help from Frederick Billings, kept Olmsted solvent as he wrapped up his Yosemite and Mariposa Estate commitments and anticipated possibly resuming his partnership with Calvert Vaux later in the fall of 1865. Vaux, who had been urging Olmsted to return East for almost two years, redoubled his efforts. He was determined that Olmsted answer his higher calling as a landscape architect—and as Vaux's business partner.[63] Vaux felt he needed Olmsted to work alongside him on a major new commission, designing Prospect Park in Brooklyn. Vaux appealed to Olmsted's self-esteem and idealism, arguing, "There can be no doubt that together we are better fitted to take up these matters than anyone else," and "what it includes is of vital importance to the progress of the Republic . . . a direct contribution to the best interests of humanity."[64]

At the time Olmsted was also entertaining the idea of

resuming his literary career alongside E. L. Godkin as coeditor of the *Nation*. He even considered remaining longer in California. "I feel that having taken such a long jump," he wrote Vaux, "I mustn't jump back again hastily."[65] Vaux began to lose patience. "There are plenty of people to write for 'The Nation,' he admonished Olmsted, "add one more to the number if you will. There are plenty of gold mines to superintend but who is going to be the better for the Gold."[66]

As he considered his future, Olmsted prepared to gather with his fellow commissioners near Yosemite in August 1865 to present the completed report. Olmsted timed the meeting to coincide with a visit to Yosemite Valley by a party of eastern dignitaries, led by the Speaker of the House of Representatives, Schuyler Colfax. The Colfax group, on a tour of the West, included two influential journalists: Albert Richardson, a war correspondent for the *New York Tribune,* and Samuel Bowles, editor and publisher of the *Springfield Republican.* In mid-August, Olmsted met with the commissioners, who approved the Yosemite Report and then joined the Colfax group. After the whole party posed near Yosemite Falls for a photograph taken by Watkins, Olmsted read the full report to them. It was an opportunity to make his ideas known to an audience beyond California.

Both Richardson and Bowles, affected by their visit to Yosemite and by Olmsted's presentation, returned East to write popular books on their travels. They argued that the protection and promotion of the West's unique landscapes greatly enhanced America's international standing. "In exhaustlessness and variety of resources, no other country on the globe," wrote Richardson, "equals ours beyond the Mississippi. In grand natural curiosities and wonders, all other countries combined fall far below it." Richardson noted with approval that a mountain in Yosemite had been named to commemorate Thomas Starr King and suggested that El Capitan be renamed for Abraham Lincoln. He described how the new park came into being, in terms that echoed Olmsted's: "An act of Congress has segregated Yosemite valley and the Mariposa groves of Big Trees, from the general public domain, setting them apart as pleasure grounds for the people of the United States and their heirs and assigns forever." Praising the wisdom of Congress, Richardson asserted Yosemite's value as a national asset, declaring, "This wise legislation secures to the proper national uses, incomparably the largest and grandest park, and the sublimest natural scenery in the whole world." Influenced by Olmsted's recommendations, Richardson appealed to his readers to forever preserve these places, to "keep them free from mutilation, and see no vandal hand of Art attempts to improve upon the simplicity and grandeur of Nature."[67]

Samuel Bowles begins his account of visiting Yosemite with the observation that "no so limited space in all the known world offers such majestic and impressive beauty. Niagara alone divides honors with it in America." He then explained the larger context of Olmsted's vision, pointing out that "wise cession and dedication [of the Yosemite Valley] by Congress, and proposed improvement by California . . . furnishes an admirable example for other objects of natural curiosity and popular interest all over the Union." He presciently recommended, "New York should preserve for popular use both Niagara Falls and its neighborhood and a generous section of her famous Adirondacks, and Maine one of her lakes and its surrounding woods."[68]

Horace Greeley, already well acquainted with Yosemite Valley, having traveled there in 1859, further amplified the importance of the example of Yosemite Park in the pages of the

New York Tribune. In an 1868 editorial, the *Tribune* reminded its readers that the creation of the park was the "largest and noblest" act "at any time in the world's history" for the "health and enjoyment of its people; and the fact that the General Government gave the land for such a purpose . . . showed a high state of civilization." The *Tribune* emphasized that the future of the park "concerns not only the state of California but the whole of the United States; and we may well say, the whole civilized world."[69]

Despite the success of his presentation to the Colfax party, Olmsted must have felt regret as he realized that his engagement with Yosemite was now coming to a close. "I am preparing a scheme of management for the Yosemite," he had written to his father with obvious pride, "the noblest public park, or pleasure ground in the world."[70] Yosemite had provided Olmsted a national platform, just as his books on the South and his work on Central Park had done. In the report he had synthesized his theories on landscape design, social equity, human rights, public health, art, culture, parks, and the duties of government into a larger, compelling vision for a reconstructed America. This vision suggested a signature role for future national parks, inspired by Yosemite's example. The efficacy of his ideas about both national parks and remaking of American society would soon be put to the test.

THREE

NATIONAL PARKS AND
A NATIONAL PARK SERVICE

After this final visit to Yosemite Valley in August 1865, Olmsted's future appeared uncertain. A number of eastern friends tried to enlist his services in the monumental task of Southern Reconstruction now facing the country. Samuel Bowles and E. L. Godkin put forward Olmsted's name as a possible candidate for running the Freedmen's Bureau. With his rejection at Port Royal no doubt still on his mind, Olmsted demurred, desiring more autonomy and control than the government was likely prepared to give him. He worried that, much like his Sanitary Commission experience, running the Freedmen's Bureau might end up "a vexatious, aggravating and thankless duty."[1] He also declined a position as general secretary of the American Freedmen's Aid Union Commission, a nondenominational league of philanthropic relief organizations. He chose instead to resume his partnership with Calvert Vaux in New York, thus beginning a thirty-year career designing many of the most treasured parks in the country. Arriving from California in November 1865, Olmsted began work with Vaux on Prospect Park, and the two men were also reappointed as consulting landscape architects for Central Park.[2]

Back in California, Olmsted's Yosemite Park report languished without his being present to advance his ideas. Several fellow commissioners, worried that Olmsted's proposals for Yosemite might compete with budget priorities of their own, chose not to forward his recommendations to the California legislature. It has been assumed by some historians that since its specific park development recommendations were not acted on, the rest of the report was suppressed as well. This assumption implied that a great "blueprint" for national parks remained unread, discarded, or buried away in a state government file cabinet in Sacramento.[3] That is, until 1952, when Olmsted's biographer, Laura Wood Roper, published the report in *Landscape Architecture*. The copy of the Yosemite Report "discovered" by Roper on a visit to the offices of the Olmsted firm in Brookline, Massachusetts, had in fact, always been available to Frederick Law Olmsted Jr., who inherited and expanded his father's design practice. The report was never discarded or forgotten. Olmsted had used it in crafting his 1887 report on Niagara Falls. Olmsted Jr. quoted from it extensively and verbatim in his 1913 analysis of the Hetch Hetchy dam controversy and drew on the ideas and language of the Yosemite Report when he drafted parts of the 1916 act creating the National Park Service.

Despite the failure of California to carry out Olmsted's specific recommendations for Yosemite Valley, the park's creation stood out as an inspiration for other parks and reservations across the United States, just as Samuel Bowles had predicted. During the remainder of his life, Olmsted saw his park philosophy as laid out in the Yosemite Report slowly gain a foothold in America. Since his last visit to Yosemite Valley in 1865, however, the state's management of the park had faltered, and much of the development and damage that Olmsted warned against had occurred. The valley floor was logged to provide lumber for hotels and other tourist accommodations. Without the addition of an improved road back to the Stockton docks that Olmsted had advocated, food and pasturage had to be supplied by draining, cultivating, and fencing the valley's delicate meadows.[4]

A fierce political battle erupted in the late 1860s, when the California legislature approved the grandfathering of private homestead claims in Yosemite Valley. Recognizing that the 1864 Yosemite Grant was made in the name of the entire nation, California referred this contentious issue to Congress to resolve. Olmsted, fully occupied with eastern projects, had formally resigned from the Yosemite Commission two years earlier in 1866, but he now felt compelled to make a statement. In 1868 he published an extended excerpt from the Yosemite Report in the *New York Evening Post* and petitioned Congress to reject this attempted privatization.[5] Horace Greeley's *New York Tribune* recommended that Congress might wish to reconsider its conditional trust of Yosemite to California and assume a more direct role in the park's management. "If Californians do not see their own interests more clearly, and it they do not respect the rights of the whole country," the editorial contended, "it is the bounden duty of Congress to protect us in the possession of this most splendid of Nature's gifts to the American people."[6] Olmsted may have had a hand in drafting the *Tribune* editorial, but in any case, he and Greeley were of the same mind on the subject. The U.S. Supreme Court ultimately reaffirmed the primacy of the 1864 Yosemite Act, finding that the unsurveyed homestead claims were a clear violation of the purpose of the act and were, in the words of Justice Stephen Field, who delivered the high court's opinion, a "perversion of the trust solemnly accepted by the State."[7]

Olmsted was also following postwar developments in the South. His hopes that the defeat of the Confederacy and ending of slavery would bring about reunification and reconstruction of the nation in the spirit of the Yosemite Report were quickly dashed by President Andrew Johnson. Olmsted had nothing but scorn for Lincoln's successor. When Johnson returned control of the Southern state governments to the same white elites that had ruled them before and during the war, Olmsted predicted that the re-empowerment of former Confederates would have dire consequences for newly emancipated Blacks. "We cannot safely hand over the negroes nor can we risk the national welfare," Olmsted wrote in 1866, "by giving the degree of responsibility to the whole body of whites of the South."[8]

Olmsted had foreseen, as early as 1863, that vanquished Confederates would retrench and continue to defend their grip on power even after final Union victory. With remarkable foresight he had warned that pro-Reconstruction officeholders in the South "will be in danger of assassination and all manner of . . . obstruction." He also cautioned Northern and Southern Union loyalists to forswear any quick reconciliation with their former enemies, that a just peace could only be achieved by "gradual wearing out, dying off and killing-off" of the most intransigent rebels.[9] He was not alone in his apprehension. George Perkins Marsh wrote the Harvard art historian Charles Eliot Norton at the time, "I never feared the war. I have always feared and still fear the peace."[10]

In 1867, Olmsted volunteered to serve as an officer of the New York–based Southern Famine Relief Commission alongside several former Sanitary Commission colleagues. Operating for less than a year, the commission was established to supply food to destitute white and Black communities in war-ravaged Southern states. Olmsted wrote the commission's final close-out report, dutifully tallying funds raised and bushels of corn sent South, but also appended a cautionary comment about stalled Reconstruction efforts. "It remains to be seen," he noted, "whether the war, which has cost us so much, has, after all, brought us nearer in our public or our private life to the divine requirement: 'Do unto others as ye would that they should do unto you.'"[11]

Olmsted welcomed congressional intervention to stop President Johnson's efforts to thwart Reconstruction, intervention that eventually led to Johnson's impeachment and very nearly to his removal from office. After Ulysses S. Grant was elected president in 1868, a series of Reconstruction Enforcement Acts were passed by Congress to suppress white supremacist violence in the South that threatened the hard-fought gains of Union victory, including equal rights and Black political enfranchisement. The ratification of the Fourteenth and Fifteenth Amendments to the Constitution represented an unprecedented expansion of federal jurisdiction over civil rights and for a time appeared to guarantee African Americans, North and South, birthright citizenship, equal protection before the law, and male suffrage. Biracial, Republican-led state governments took power in many Southern states. It seemed that the promise of a reconstructed nation might yet be realized.

Olmsted, still unable to shake his old paternalism, worried that freedmen needed more preparation to exercise full suffrage. On the contrary, Southern Blacks demonstrated that they were ready for participatory democracy and holding elected office. Whatever his reservations, Olmsted supported adoption of the Fourteenth Amendment. He had always believed that "the war should not be merely for the Union but for a Union without slavery." Now he believed "it is not the abolition of slavery that is required to be decreed as the condition of peace but the abolition of class and caste before the law."[12] Years later Supreme Court Justice John Marshall Harlan would use similar language in his famous *Plessy v. Ferguson* dissent attacking the 1896 Court decision that nationally codified the segregation of races.[13] "In the view of the Constitution, in the eye of the law," Harlan wrote, "there is in this country no superior, dominant, ruling class of citizens. There is no caste here."[14] Speaking before the American Freedmen's Union Commission in 1866, Olmsted's former benefactor Frederick Billings rhetorically asked his audience how the emancipated should be treated. "I answer, precisely as we would treat four million white men . . . who themselves had been enslaved all their lives," Billings replied. "Treat them as human beings, with rights to be protected, with faculties to be developed, with lives to be made useful."[15]

The abandonment and eventual collapse of Southern Reconstruction has been attributed to half measures that did not enable freedpeople to make a safe transition from slavery to citizenship.[16] Federal power, invigorated by the war, had been marshaled to end slavery, reunify the country, and pass new laws for education, railroads, Western settlement, and even parks. Political will, however, faltered when it came to sustaining Reconstruction, overcoming organized white paramilitary resistance and protecting the rights of the South's newly enfranchised Black citizens. The enforcement of hard-won civil rights statutes and related constitutional protections was repeatedly blocked in the Supreme Court. When federal troops and marshals in the South were directed to stand down, African Americans, faced with overwhelming white supremacist violence, fought to defend their rights for as long as they could. "The public seems to have tired of the subject," wrote the Ohio Republican congressman and future president James Garfield, "and all appeals to do justice to the Negro."[17] "Former Confed-

erates," explained one scholar, "would easily outlast a northern populace eager to move on and grapple with the mounting
problems of an industrial age."[18]

So it seemed that over time Olmsted's attention shifted as
well. His famine relief report would mark the end of his involvement in the future of African Americans in the South. In step
with the shifting mood of the nation, his interest in the drawn-
out struggle over Southern Reconstruction began to wane. He
joined the ranks of many Northerners who—satisfied that
civil rights laws now existed, at least on paper—turned their
attention to national reconciliation and their business interests,
including restoration of commercial ties to the South. It was,
as Olmsted had once written to his friend Frederick Knapp,
"enough for us."

In fact, there is no record of Olmsted's commenting on the
subject of civil rights until 1889, when he was asked by a Southern business acquaintance, Thomas Clark, for his opinion on
the "relics of slavery." At the time, Olmsted's Brookline office
was consulting with the "redeemed" segregationist government
of Alabama on a possible plan for the state capitol grounds in
Montgomery. Clark, an official in the governor's office, was
aware of Olmsted's earlier publications and asked for his views
"because your books on the South made me curious."[19] In an
equivocal, if not dissembling, letter back to Clark, Olmsted
struggled to square the strong antislavery orientation of his
early writings with his growing detachment from the current
racial realities of the South.

Olmsted stated that Black suffrage was viewed as necessary
during Reconstruction to assure that there would be no return
to "quasi-slavery or political subordination." But he assured
Clark that he always believed full political rights for freedpeople should have been granted conditionally, as "a privilege to

be earned." He praised the South's "amazing" economic recovery and new prosperity and made the astonishing claim that Blacks "have done a great deal better . . . than I ever imagined it possible." There are people in the North, Olmsted still cautioned, who are worried "that the whites of the South are not 'playing fair' about the negroes at elections." But he conceded, without any justification, that this was "for a time, to a large degree, inevitable." He ended his letter wishfully appealing to the "more intelligent people of the South to struggle out of it [suppressing the Black vote] as fast as possible"—a forlorn hope reminiscent of the widely shared delusion during the Civil War that many white Southerners were loyal at heart and would eventually rally to the Union in a moment of national deliverance.[20] Sadly, Olmsted's ill-informed optimism notwithstanding, the disenfranchisement of African American voters in Alabama, and many other Southern states, would continue for a further seventy-five years. Not until the 1965 Selma-to-Montgomery March and sustained protests by African Americans did the enactment and enforcement of the Voting Rights Act compel the State of Alabama to "play fair" at elections.

In any case, after 1865, Olmsted's career as a landscape architect demanded all his time and energy. His writing and efforts increasingly concentrated on his activities as a landscape designer and park advocate. His concern for social justice had not disappeared, but was expressed through his professional work. His "landscape work," as Laura Wood Roper observed, "was to become increasingly the channel through which he satisfied that urge for social usefulness." As Olmsted himself confessed, "My enthusiasm and liking for the work is increasing to an inconvenient degree, so that it elbows all other interests out of my mind."[21] Olmsted's idea for national parks, the "great public grounds for the free enjoyment of the people," gained momentum, even as the landscape architect himself was now preoccupied with building a professional practice and designing major municipal parks. This was the true legacy of the Yosemite Report. Ironically, the emerging national parks movement required neither the direct involvement of the report's author nor the implementation of his management plan for Yosemite. Individuals were soon applying ideas from the report in different places around the country. The next step in federal park making came in 1872, when Congress set aside two million acres of land in the Montana and Wyoming Territories to create Yellowstone National Park.

Congress, at the height of Southern Reconstruction, believed it was empowered to attempt things never thought possible, including the creation of a national park. It set up new bureaucracies including the Justice Department, the Pension Office, the Freedmen's Bureau, and a system of national cemeteries.[22] "Execution of these newly recognized responsibilities," wrote the historian Drew Gilpin Faust, "would prove an important vehicle for the expansion of federal power that characterized the transformed postwar nation." Faust described how these new responsibilities were "of a scale and reach unimaginable before the war."[23] The historian Adam Wesley Dean places the Yellowstone Act in a continuum of Republican legislative actions that upended the prewar political status quo. "All of these measures," Dean pointed out—including the 1866 Civil Rights Act, the 1867 Reconstruction Acts, passage of the Fourteenth and Fifteenth Amendments to the Constitution, and the 1871 Ku Klux Klan Act—"would have been unthinkable in antebellum America."[24]

Key Republican sponsors of the Yellowstone Park legislation included Illinois senator Lyman Trumbull, Kansas senator Samuel Pomeroy, and Massachusetts representative Henry Dawes; all had voted for the Yosemite Act and were early architects and supporters of Reconstruction. In addition, Lyman Trumbull had sponsored the Thirteenth Amendment, the first Freedmen's Bureau Bill, and the Civil Rights Act. As they crafted the bill for Yellowstone, they looked to the Yosemite Act for inspiration. "Yosemite was Yellowstone's model," wrote the historian Alfred Runte. "Similar to Yosemite Valley and the Mariposa Redwood Grove, Yellowstone was 'dedicated and set apart as a public park or pleasuring ground for the benefit and enjoyment of the people.'"[25] The similarity between the two pieces of park legislation was striking. Even the moving imagery of Thomas Moran's paintings and William Henry Jackson's photographs of Yellowstone evoked Bierstadt's and Watkins's earlier contributions to the Yosemite preservation campaign.

Since Montana and Wyoming were territories, the option of placing Yellowstone under state administration was foreclosed. But Congress was predisposed, in any event, to create a "national park" under federal, rather than state or territorial administration. The designation of a national park, in the era of Reconstruction, was concomitant with rising public expectations for the national government. Framers of the Yellowstone legislation were also well aware of California's shortcomings in managing Yosemite. The contested action on preemption claims in Yosemite Valley was still being adjudicated by the Supreme Court when the Yellowstone bill was being drafted. Referring to the Yosemite preemption dispute, Senators Pomeroy and Trumbull wanted to ensure that such uncertainty would never cloud Yellowstone's future. "We did set apart the region of the country on which the mammoth trees grow in

California, and the Yosemite Valley also we have undertaken to reserve," affirmed Trumbull on the floor of the Senate, "but there is a dispute about it. Now, before there is any dispute as to this wonderful country, I hope we shall except it from the general disposition of the public lands, and reserve it to the Government."[26]

Congress was ready to accept the idea of establishing Yellowstone as a national reservation, managing it, as Olmsted had earlier argued for Yosemite, as a "duty of government." The legislation was passed by Congress with the support of a sizable Republican majority, and on March 1, 1872, President Grant signed an act creating Yellowstone National Park. The *Nation* predicted just days later that "the act of Congress setting aside the Yellowstone region as a national park . . . will help confirm the national possession of the Yo Semite, and may in time lead us to rescue Niagara."[27]

If the move to create Yellowstone National Park was far-sighted, two aspects of congressional action on Yellowstone were not. Native Americans, once again, were erased from the wilderness park tableau. There were no advocates in Washington for Indigenous bands, including the Shoshone, Bannock, and Crow, who seasonally hunted in Yellowstone. Congress also failed to make any provision for the management of this vast new park. Neither staff nor funding were provided for many years. Yellowstone National Park, by default, had been placed under the jurisdiction of the Interior Department, an underfunded and disordered agency charged with caring for a growing roster of federal lands. The department could not field an effective administrative structure to prevent the depredation of park features and wildlife by early visitors.[28] The solution was to bridge the gap between legislative ambition and executive capacity by turning to the United States Army, the only institution of government that was reasonably organized and trained for such a task.

The Civil War had transformed the army into a multipurpose instrument for carrying out national policy, as it did for a time during Reconstruction. During this postwar period, the military became, in the words of the historian Richard White, an "armed bureaucracy," and army officers were seconded to "administer Indian reservations, staff the Freedmen's Bureau, [and] police new national parks."[29] Military administration of Yellowstone began in 1886 and was expanded in the 1890s to include Sierran national parks: Sequoia, General Grant (Kings Canyon), and Yosemite. Many of these early park military guardians were Civil War veterans and included African American cavalrymen, who became known as Buffalo Soldiers. In 1903, Colonel Charles Young, a West Point graduate whose parents had been enslaved, became superintendent of Sequoia National Park. The army remained in national parks for almost thirty years.

Olmsted did not foresee in the 1865 Yosemite Report how the government would eventually have to reorganize itself to adequately manage and protect a growing portfolio of parks as a "duty of government." But he intuitively understood that Yosemite not only represented a revolutionary idea about the efficacy, design, and governance of large scenic parks but also manifested a government functioning as it never had before. Olmsted also could not have foreseen the West's phenomenal postwar transformation with the explosive exploitation of natural resources, most notably large-scale deforestation. But the example of Yosemite Valley took on new significance with mounting concern that more of these great scenic landscapes must be reserved for the benefit of the American people. The historian Lisa Brady has examined the transition from a government that moved all public land into private ownership to a government that assumed responsibility for managing a growing share of the remaining public domain. "The war did not upend Americans' relationships with or ideas about nature," she observed, "but instead provided the rationale for broadening and expanding them to include nature protection at the national level. The war that established federal authority over states' rights to determine citizenship and other civil rights also established increased federal power to decide what elements in the natural treasury would become permanent fixtures of the national landscape."[30] However tentative the start, the contours of a "national landscape" were beginning to take shape and a fledgling national parks movement was launched.

Olmsted was not involved in these early national park affairs, although he was aware of them. By the early 1880s he had relocated to Brookline, Massachusetts, where he created a home and office he called Fairsted. There, he undertook many of the most important commissions of his career, including his most significant and fully developed municipal park system, created for the city of Boston. The practice grew and diversified as he trained a new generation of landscape architects in the office, including his stepson, John Charles Olmsted, and Charles Eliot. His friend and sometime collaborator Charles Sprague Sargent was a neighbor. The founding director of Harvard's Arnold Arboretum, Sargent was the author of the first comprehensive survey of American forests. He also promoted the establishment of a federal forest reserve system and the Forest Reserve Act of 1891, which authorized the president to establish "public reservations" on any forested federal lands.[31] Sargent helped draft the 1892 legislation for Adirondack Park, created by the State of New York, and he advocated for the establishment of Glacier National Park in Montana. Through

Sargent as well as many other contacts and correspondents, Olmsted was aware of the developments in national park making that he had been so influential in initiating. His own contributions to scenic preservation during this period, however, would be in the East and through state and local, not federal, park projects.

Niagara Falls, on the border with Canada in upstate New York, had been the original symbol of America's scenic grandeur—the standard against which Yosemite had been judged. But the land adjacent to the falls had remained in private hands, and for decades the spectacle had been surrounded by unsightly tourist and industrial development that restricted access and marred views. This unfortunate precedent was well known to those concerned with the fate of scenic areas of the West. Samuel Bowles's recommendation that Yosemite be used as a model to remedy conditions at Niagara Falls expressed a common sentiment, one shared by Olmsted among others. This interest intensified in the late 1860s when Olmsted began designing Buffalo's park system and where he joined a growing citizens' movement in that city to reclaim the nearby falls.

In 1879 the New York legislature appointed Olmsted and James Gardner, director of the New York State Survey, to prepare a special report on conditions at the falls and to make recommendations on how to improve them.[32] Olmsted and Gardner emphasized the need to acquire the landscape setting of the falls, not just the cataract itself, in order to create an experience worthy of the natural spectacle. Knowing that the political obstacles to the unprecedented (for a state government) action of creating such a park, Olmsted began one of the earliest public relations campaigns for such a purpose. Advocacy groups, influential individuals, and corporations had backed the Yosemite and Yellowstone Acts, but at Niagara, Olmsted sought to generate a broader public constituency that would influence legislators.

With his friend Charles Eliot Norton, Olmsted circulated a petition, signed by many leading cultural and political leaders in the United States as well as Canada, urging the State of New York to act. Many of the signatories were associates from Olmsted's early literary career, his service during the Civil War with the Sanitary Commission, and his work on the Yosemite Report.[33] Building on this petition, Olmsted and Norton helped form the Niagara Falls Association to lead a citizens' campaign for Niagara's preservation. Olmsted and Norton also hired the journalists Henry Norman and Jonathan Harrison to write articles decrying the existing condition of the area. Olmsted had never been reticent about influencing popular opinion and had long been an active promoter of his causes. But the movement supporting a Niagara reservation represented a new era of public conservation advocacy. Success came in 1883, when the legislature passed a bill to establish the Niagara Reservation and Governor Grover Cleveland (former mayor of Buffalo and future president) signed it. In 1885 funds were finally appropriated to establish the reservation, the first park of its type to be created by a state government. In 1886, Olmsted, working once again with his former partner Calvert Vaux, designed a new park around Niagara Falls.[34]

Olmsted saw his plans for Niagara come to fruition, but the management of Yosemite Valley had taken a different and contrasting direction. While the park remained a public property, the haphazard and heavy-handed development of Yosemite Valley was exactly what he had hoped to avoid. No one, Olmsted included, had appreciated how much of the valley landscape had been shaped by human activity long before white settlement. Tribal groups who had made Yosemite their home for millennia periodically set fires to improve game habitat, increase acorn production, and keep the landscape open. The result was the "beautiful" and parklike valley landscape Olmsted had so admired. But once it became a park, fire suppression was considered a fundamental necessity for its protection. By the 1880s, afforestation of the valley floor began to reduce the size of the meadows, cut off views of geological features, and generally change the character of the landscape. Flood control measures, increasingly necessary to protect buildings, also changed the moisture regimes and therefore the vegetation of the meadows. Hotel operators and park commissioners responded by pruning or removing the lodge pole pines that proliferated with the absence of fire in drier soils.

But for park and wilderness advocates, now including the naturalist John Muir and Robert Underwood Johnson, the influential editor of *Century* magazine, cutting trees seemed inimical to the preservation of wilderness. Muir and Johnson spent two weeks camping in Yosemite in 1889 and were of like mind regarding what they considered the mismanagement of the valley by state authorities. Their initial campaign, to establish a much larger Yosemite National Park surrounding the state reservation, would succeed the following year, in 1890. Turning their attention to Yosemite Valley, Johnson wrote to Olmsted describing what he considered its deplorable condition, especially regarding the removal of trees.[35] Twenty-four years after Olmsted presented his Yosemite Report, Johnson hoped he would return again as a consultant to the Yosemite Commission, or at the very least join their protest.

Olmsted, however, was bound to have a more positive attitude toward the necessity of tree thinning in park landscapes. By 1889 he had designed dozens of parks that required the planting of thousands of trees and shrubs. Best practice called for planting thick and thinning later. But removing trees could often alarm members of the public who perceived it as destructive, especially when done badly. The same year Johnson wrote to him regarding Yosemite Valley, Olmsted was drawn into a controversy over the thinning of the maturing stands of trees in Central Park. Working again with Jonathan Harrison, he published *Observations on the Treatment of Public Plantations, More Especially relating to the Use of the Axe.*[36] The two authors assembled opinions from leading horticulturists to support the contention that thinning was a necessary aspect of the maintenance of tree plantations. Olmsted therefore replied to Johnson only after considerable reflection. Though he knew the management of the valley needed improvement, he was unwilling to condemn tree removal without better knowledge of the situation. "All I could say," he wrote to Johnson, "is that, having at an early day spent several months in the valley under peculiarly favorable circumstances for contemplating it, I know that the question is one of far greater importance and of far greater difficulty than can be generally realized." Olmsted wanted to take a longer view of the issue, writing, "It is most foolish to take it up in an occasional and desultory way as a question of details, or as a question the answer to which will be chiefly important to the people of the present century. It is preeminently a question of our duty to the future."[37]

As a result of his growing practice—and the opportunities presented by an expanding national rail system—Olmsted traveled to California three times in the 1880s, but he never returned to Yosemite Valley. Certainly he was busy with his professional commitments, especially the design of the Stanford University campus. He also may not have wanted to see the results of the state's mismanagement. But he was finally drawn into the controversy the next year, in 1890, when he published a pamphlet at his own expense, *Governmental Preservation of Natural Scenery.*[38] After giving an account of his early involvement with Yosemite, he pointed out that tree thinning should be done, in any park, only according to plans and procedures drawn up by those who were qualified to do so. He included a quotation from the Niagara report he and Vaux had completed three years earlier, which he felt should also serve as guidance for Yosemite policy: "Nothing of an artificial character should be allowed a place on the property . . . no matter how valuable it might be under other circumstances, and no matter at how little cost it may be had, the presence of which can be avoided consistently with the provision of necessary conditions for making the enjoyment of the natural scenery available." However, Olmsted once more refused to criticize the commissioners, repeating again that he had not made a thorough study of their policies.

John Muir, likely unhappy about sharing the Yosemite limelight with the famous Olmsted, was not impressed by the pamphlet. "Mr. Olmsted's paper," Muir wryly commented, "was, I thought, a little soft in some places."[39] In fairness to Olmsted, it had been more than twenty years since he was directly involved with Yosemite. It may be that his peripatetic work life, as he once said, "elbows all other interests out of my mind." It may also be that he looked at scenic preservation in the valley and the need for minimal professional design intervention—but intervention all the same—from a different perspective than the totally hands-off Muir. In any event, Olmsted was in the final years of his career and for any number of reasons, including perhaps being mindful of other projects and clients in California, he chose once again not to take sides on Yosemite.

By the early 1890s, Olmsted's health had begun to fail. His influence on the American parks movement continued and was carried forward and enlarged through his mentorship of several of the most important landscape architects and planners of the late nineteenth and early twentieth centuries. Chief among these was his son, Frederick Law Olmsted Jr., whose education and training were of particular concern to his father, and Charles Eliot, who was recruited by Olmsted, in 1883, as an apprentice. Eliot is best known for organizing the first private land trust, the Trustees of Public Reservations. Established through an act of the Massachusetts state legislature in 1891, the Trustees accepted gifts of land to be held (tax free) and kept open to the public. Eliot's concept of a unified regional system of scenic reservations suggested a model for organizing and managing a national park system. Eliot also recognized, as Olmsted had, that larger scenic reservations demanded a balance of landscape development, forest management, and preservation of natural features. When Olmsted retired in 1895, Eliot was a partner in the Fairsted firm. His sudden death in 1897, however, deprived the office and the nation of one of the country's most important conservation and park thinkers. With Eliot's passing, it remained for the young Olmsted Jr. to assume this role, now as a new partner in the reorganized firm of Olmsted Brothers.

The development of the national park system has often been characterized as a progressive narrative in which the country inevitably gained conservation wisdom and insight as one new national park after another was created. But progress was not preordained; each step would be contested and on occasion reversed. Given competing priorities, legislative indifference, and the absence of administrative capacity and leadership,

Congress moved cautiously on new park proposals. In addition there was a deep-seated ambivalence about government's role in creating, protecting, and managing large national reservations. Legislation to establish Crater Lake National Park required fourteen bills introduced over a sixteen-year period before the park was finally authorized in 1902.[40] When Congress did establish a new park, legislators often failed to provide staffing, management tools, and funding. One description of this postwar period as a "bumpy and nonlinear course of change" could certainly be applied to the early development of national parks.[41]

But the political environment was changing. A new civic culture taking root across turn-of-the-century America led to the rise of national advocacy organizations. Americans by the millions joined leagues, lodges, clubs, and unions. Those taking a strong interest in national parks included conservationists, outdoor groups, hunters, and railroad and tourism business interests. Railroad executives expected new national parks to attract tourists who would ride their trains and stay in their hotels. They exercised considerable political influence, as did elite Boone and Crockett clubs, representing wealthy sportsmen concerned with wildlife depredation. As a growing middle class became more politically active, new advocates for national parks emerged, including a number of reform-minded women.

Many of these civic reformers saw national parks as instruments of modernity and social progress, and they shared the Yosemite Report's expectation that great parks would enhance the public's health and general welfare. Mary Belle King Sherman, president of the Federation of Women's Clubs (representing three thousand clubs across the country) believed national parks to be an amalgamation of treasured civic institutions, possessing "some of the characteristics of the museum, the library, the fine arts hall, and the public school."[42] J. Horace McFarland, president of the American Civic Association, concurred. "Everything that the limited scope of a city park can do as quick aid to the citizen," he explained, national parks "are ready to do more thoroughly, on a greater scale."[43] Left out of this movement, however, were working people, including people of color who received few benefits from the national parks and other Western public lands.

Park supporters did have the advantage of congressional precedents already in place—first the Yosemite Grant and then Yellowstone. A small but growing number of sympathetic members of Congress were vital to the advancement of the national park cause. Missouri senator George Vest and Tennessee senator William Bate, two former Confederate officers, were ardent Yellowstone supporters. Turning back an attempt to substantially cut the size of Yellowstone in the 1890s, Bate reminded his colleagues: "Yellowstone National Park is a reservation set apart by the Government for the people in common. . . . I do not desire to see it diverted from the original intention. . . . I look upon it," he declared, "as I do upon the reservation of Yosemite Valley and of the big trees in Mariposa Grove."[44] Vest repeatedly tried to provide Yellowstone with administrative authority to enforce park rules and protect its threatened resources, notably the park's fragile thermal features. His legislation repeatedly passed the Senate only to fail in the House, until Iowa congressman John Lacey, a former Union Army major, assumed the chairmanship of the House Committee on Public Lands. Lacey maneuvered the Yellowstone National Park Protection Act, also known as the Lacey Act of 1894, through the recalcitrant House. The act established park rules that could be enforced by the U.S.

District Court of Wyoming. Similar authorities were later enacted by Congress for Yosemite, Sequoia, and General Grant National Parks. For the first time, an administrative framework was approved laying the cornerstone for professional management of national parks.

Lacey led the fight for the passage of the 1906 Antiquities Act, which protected the nation's interest in safeguarding sites of archaeological and historical significance as well as scenic places. Congress had already demonstrated a similar motivation, creating commemorative parks on former Civil War battlefields to be managed by the War Department. The Antiquities Act further established a clear and systematic process for the executive branch to expand, through presidential proclamation, the domain of the national park system. Perhaps most important, it gave the president far-reaching authority to protect not only prehistoric ruins but also public land that possessed "scientific or historic interest." Despite Lacey's assurances that each application of the act would apply to the "smallest area compatible" with its purposes, Theodore Roosevelt issued national monument proclamations for the 800,000-acre Grand Canyon, the Petrified Forest, and many other large Western landscapes.[45] Many of the monuments established under the antiquities law, such as Crater Lake, Grand Canyon, and Mount Olympus, would eventually be redesignated by Congress as national parks.

The historian Richard West Sellars considered the passage of the 1906 Antiquities Act a watershed moment for the nascent national park system. "In the realm of historic and natural preservation on the nation's public lands," Sellars asserted, "no law had ever approached the scope of the 1906 Antiquities Act. Much more broadly than legislation enabling individual national parks, the act made explicit that preservation of historic, archeological, and other scientific sites on lands controlled by the federal government was indeed a federal respon-sibility."[46] But this could have been an even greater watershed moment if Lacey had managed to pass an earlier version of the antiquities legislation, which had been recommended by Bin-ger Hermann, commissioner of the General Land Office. H.R. 11021, "A Bill to establish and administer national parks," would have given the president the authority to create all future national parks by proclamation. "Since Congress has empow-ered the President to set apart tracts of public land for forest-reservation purposes," Hermann explained in his department's 1901 annual report to Congress, " . . . it appears altogether rea-sonable . . . that the same power should be vested in the Pres-ident in respect to reserving tracts of public land for national park purposes."[47] Lacey agreed, believing that the time had come for professional, unified national park administration—a national park service. Although H.R. 11021 failed to pass, the 1906 Antiquities Act in its final form still granted the executive branch expansive new powers to set aside and protect public lands under permanent federal management. The contours of the modern national park system were beginning to emerge, but it would take another eleven years for Congress to create a professional national park service.[48]

In 1910, President William Howard Taft signed the Gla-cier National Park Act into law and the following year sent a message to Congress endorsing the establishment of a pro-fessional bureau to oversee the nation's growing portfolio of national parks and monuments. In his message, drawing heav-ily on themes articulated in Olmsted's Yosemite Report, Taft requested funding to "bring all these natural wonders within easy reach of the people," enhancing their "accessibility and usefulness." He believed that the national parks required a gov-ernment bureau distinctly charged with their management and development. Such a bureau would protect the parks and fulfill "an obligation of the government to preserve them for the edification and recreation of the people."[49]

The influence of Frederick Law Olmsted (who died in 1903 after a long illness) on national park development would be amplified through the training and preparation he had given his son. The younger Olmsted was uniquely qualified to move the nineteenth-century park movement into the twentieth century. He officially entered the family firm in 1895, the year his father retired, and two years later, at the age of twenty-seven, became a full partner with his older half-brother, John Charles. Olmsted Jr. went on to lead the firm for decades as the nation's foremost authority on landscape architecture and a direct link to the ideas and practice of his father. He was particularly active as an adviser in the management of Yosemite Valley. His involvement began in the early twentieth century when a proposal was made to dam the Tuolumne River through the Hetch Hetchy Valley in Yosemite National Park.[50]

The national park encircling Yosemite Valley had been established in 1890. In 1906, California finally "receded" the original Yosemite Grant back to the federal government, incorporating Yosemite Valley and Mariposa Grove into the national park as Johnson and Muir, among others, had long urged. Since the San Francisco earthquake and fire of 1906, however, municipal interests had begun advocating for the use of Yosemite National Park to provide a reliable source of water for the city, even if it meant building a dam in the park. Hetch Hetchy Valley, not far from Yosemite Valley, rivaled it in the eyes of many as a greater scenic wonder. But the larger issue at stake was setting a precedent for keeping national parks free from such development to prevent their being available—like the forest reserves—for the construction of dams and reservoirs.

The Hetch Hetchy proposal set off a bitter national debate that split the national park coalition in California. Much to Muir's anguish, even the Sierra Club divided on the issue. Municipal officials rallied support from wealthy and influential outdoorsmen and conservationists sympathetic to civic improvements. Opposition to the dam by national park defenders galvanized into a nationwide crusade endorsed by civic organizations across the country. J. Horace McFarland and the noted poet Harriet Monroe joined the Sierra Club and Appalachian Mountain Club to forge an East-West anti-dam alliance, the Society for the Preservation of National Parks. At its biannual conventions in 1908 and 1910, the 800,000-member Federation of Women's Clubs went on record opposing the flooding of Hetch Hetchy Valley. "We are earnestly opposed to such a needless local use of a priceless national possession in which the entire citizenship is interested," petitioned the Grafort Club of Portsmouth, New Hampshire, one of 150 women's clubs that appealed to their elected representatives to stop the dam.[51] The ensuing battle extended over three presidential administrations and five Interior secretaries and was finally left to Congress to sort out.

Olmsted Jr., a friend of McFarland and a member of the American Civic Association, spoke out for himself and for his father's legacy. In 1913, as a congressional decision on Hetch Hetchy neared, he offered his assessment of what he thought was at stake. In a piece for the *Boston Evening Transcript,* he quoted from his father's analysis of Yosemite's scenic beauty taken directly from the purportedly lost Yosemite Report. Asserting that the construction of a dam in a national park violated the reasons for creating it, as his father had set them out almost fifty years earlier, he argued that the park should retain "the landscape qualities which, in all the world, are peculiar to Yosemite scenery . . . and which in the next few centuries will, I believe, become of incalculably larger value to humanity." He described the policy as an increasingly vital imperative, as unspoiled scenery was becoming increasingly scarce. "The lesson of history in this respect is unmistakable," he concluded; a place of "great and peculiar beauty, and which cannot be replaced," should not be destroyed "even if the predominant men of the day fail to appreciate its beauty." Some places were "of a value wholly or primarily for their beauty, and if they have any direct utilitarian value it is utterly secondary and incidental. If we can afford it, we direct our efforts toward conserving and making available its primary value, its beauty."[52]

The predominant men of the day finally did make up their minds. In December 1913 the act authorizing the Hetch Hetchy dam was finally approved by Congress. A broad agreement emerged, however, that there had to be a better way to deal with future national park controversies. Olmsted Jr. and others advocated for an organized, professional, and uniform approach to park development and operations to replace the haphazard establishment and management of national parks up to that point. "The present situation in regard to the national parks is very bad," Olmsted Jr. contended. "They have been created one at a time by acts of Congress which have not defined at all clearly the purposes for which the lands were to be set apart, nor provided any orderly or efficient means of safeguarding the parks."[53] McFarland echoed this bleak assessment. "The parks have just happened," he wrote in the *Sierra Club Bulletin;* "they are not the result of such an overlooking of the national domain as would, and ought to, result in a coordinated system." He emphasized the need for a professional national parks bureau. "There is no adequately organized control of the national parks. With forty-one national parks and monuments, aggregating an area larger than two sovereign states, and containing priceless glories of scenery and wonders of nature, we do not have as efficient a provision for administration as is possessed by many a city of but fifty thousand inhabitants for its hundred or so acres! . . . Nowhere in official Washington can an inquirer find an office of the national parks, or a desk devoted solely to their management."[54] Shortly after the passage of the Hetch Hetchy Act, the losing side, led by McFarland, began contacting President Wilson's administration. As John Muir, who died the following year, bitterly declared, "Some sort of compensation must surely come out of even this dark damn-dam-damnation."[55]

The movement to create a federal park bureau indeed gained traction after 1913, and it would fall to Olmsted Jr. to draft the key portions of the legislation that would eventually pass in 1916. Throughout the process, he would repeatedly refer to elements of the 1865 Yosemite Report as a touchstone for the new agency and its mission. The genealogy was clear: the younger Olmsted brought experience and credentials as the foremost park planner of his day; but above all, he embodied the link to the ideas and rhetoric of his father and the 1865 report, which infused draft legislation for a new National Park Service. There were many contributing authors besides Olmsted Jr., most notably, his close collaborator McFarland, California congressman William Kent, the former newspaper editor and publicist Robert Sterling Yard, Robert Marshall, chief geographer of the U.S. Geological Survey, and Horace Albright, Stephen Mather's able assistant. Mather, a charismatic and socially well connected businessman, had been brought to Washington by the Wilson administration to oversee existing national parks and monuments and build support for a professional national park service. But it was Olmsted

Jr. who articulated and wrote the proposed agency's critical statement of purpose.[56]

In 1910, Representative Kent had encouraged Franklin Pierce, then acting secretary of the Interior, to forward an early version of park legislation to Olmsted Jr. for review and comment. The landscape architect noted that legislative language used to authorize many of the already existing national parks had "omissions and defects" that could be exploited to their detriment, as in the case of the Hetch Hetchy dam. It simply was not enough to say that no park uses shall be permitted contrary to their congressionally defined purposes. He insisted that national park service legislation must contain a stronger "general definition of purpose" that applied to all existing and future national parks—language that he provided. Olmsted Jr.'s statement of purpose has stood the test of time, expressing the mandate and philosophy of the new service: "The fundamental purpose" of the national parks is "to conserve the scenery and the natural and historic objects and the wild life therein and to provide for the enjoyment of the same in such manner and by such means as will leave them unimpaired for the enjoyment of future generations." According to McFarland, Olmsted Jr.'s language was "jealously preserved with much fighting and effort." Wilson signed "an Act to establish a National Park Service" on August 25, 1916.

It can be said that the intellectual path to the 1916 act began with the 1865 Yosemite Report and continued through Olmsted's municipal and metropolitan park systems, the Niagara Falls project, Eliot's work on regional scenic reservations, and back once more to Yosemite with Olmsted Jr.'s critique of the Hetch Hetchy dam. Olmsted Jr. wrote of the national parks that what made the deepest impression on him was that they were public parks. The "priceless recreational quality of these great reservations" was "to know that one is free, of his own right as human being, . . . unfenced . . . by the vexing artificial web of property rights."[57] The principle of universal public access and use of parks was at the heart of the 1865 Yosemite Report. The report made the case that Yosemite Valley was preserved for "popular resort and recreation," the "free enjoyment of the people," the "benefit of the entire nation," and for the protection of "all its citizens in the pursuit of happiness." In less evocative but no less effective language, the 1916 National Park Service Organic Act speaks to the "enjoyment of future generations," establishing that there will be no interference "with free access . . . by the public."

But that use and enjoyment needed to be mitigated by strong control over its potential impacts and especially over what types of development would be allowed. The elder Olmsted condemned any forms of development "markedly inharmonious with the scenery" and called for restricting any new construction "within the narrowest possible limits." At the 1916 conference of the American Society of Landscape Architects, his son endorsed (and probably wrote) a resolution regarding priorities for the new national park agency. "The need has long been felt not only for more adequate protection," it stated, ". . . but also for rendering this landscape beauty more readily enjoyable through construction in the parks of certain necessary roads and buildings for the accommodation of visitors in a way to bring minimum of injury to these primeval landscapes." None of this work should proceed, the resolution continued, without "comprehensive plans . . . [and] designs for construction" approved by "qualified expert advisors."[58] The 1916 act itself described the responsibility to "promote and regulate" the proper use of parks in ways that protect "natural curiosities, wonders, or objects of interest" and conserve "the scenery or the natural or historic objects." Olmsted Jr.'s added language about conserving these features "unimpaired for the enjoyment of future generations" mirrored his father's recommendations.

For almost four decades, Olmsted Jr. was a key adviser and mentor to the top leadership of the National Park Service.[59] By the time he retired in 1949, the national park system had added 150 new areas, including national parks, monuments, historic sites, recreation areas, seashores and lakeshores, and military battlefields. In 1928, Olmsted Jr. became a member of the newly formed Yosemite National Park Board of Expert Advisors and served as the board's first chairman. One of his last professional activities, at age eighty, was his return to the Yosemite advisory board once again in 1950 for a few more years of service, thus concluding the family's involvement with national parks in the same place where it began.

CONCLUSION

CAMPFIRE TALES

In this book we look at the origins of national parks in the United States through the lens of the broader park movement that developed in the years before the Civil War and rapidly matured under the tumultuous influences of the greatest social issues of the day, including the abolition of slavery and the preservation and remaking of the republic. The narrative is framed by the life and career of Frederick Law Olmsted, who gave words to the movement's most influential ideologies and form to its greatest creations. There are many other dimensions to this history and many other influential actors in its events and accomplishments. But Olmsted was a consistent thread, an individual whose beliefs and actions—and perhaps, on occasion, serendipity—consistently placed him where and when he could give rhetoric and shape to the most important cause of his life: the American park, in all its variations, meanings, purposes, and benefits for the health and well-being of individuals and society as a whole.

Many friends and colleagues feared that Olmsted was withdrawing from landscape architecture, public life, and the republican movement when he departed for California in

1863. He certainly had his share of reversals. He abandoned farming; the literary career that he had hoped for never really materialized; bureaucratic constraints limited his influence with Central Park; internecine conflict and exhaustion led to his resignation from the Sanitary Commission; and his mining enterprise ended in bankruptcy. Writing from California, at a low point in his professional life, cut off from the close fellowship of coworkers, he wistfully confided to Henry Bellows, "I look back upon the Sanitary Commission & the park, as upon a previous state of existence."[1] And yet, with each professional setback, his public stature seemed only to grow larger.

His journalism, while unable to provide a consistent livelihood, nevertheless had introduced him to other writers and intellectuals and began to afford him the national and even international reputation he desperately sought. His work with Calvert Vaux on Central Park quickly became, by any measure, a huge popular success and held out the promise that his partnership with Vaux might be revived. The leadership and organizational skills he honed working on Central Park and with the Sanitary Commission helped cement his image as an honest, competent, self-sacrificing administrator. Even his ruinous Mariposa Estate venture had brought him improbably to California and Yosemite Valley, where he was presented with an unforeseen opportunity to assume the leadership of the Yosemite Commission as a respected national figure with a valued transcontinental perspective. Olmsted would soon depart California to rejoin Vaux in New York and immerse himself in a myriad of assignments and commissions during a long and productive career. But though he would undertake many high-profile projects that would further enhance his reputation, none would afford him quite the same national platform as Yosemite.

Olmsted in the summer of 1865 looked forward to a strong and purposeful postwar government that would lead a renewed and reconstructed republic. Such a government, he hoped, would bring democracy and freedom to the South and accomplish great civic projects such as the creation of magnificent parks like Central Park and Yosemite. The kind of utopian state that Olmsted fervently hoped for, however, did not come to pass. His optimism about enlightened government began to fade almost as soon as Andrew Johnson ascended to the presidency, perhaps even before the Yosemite Report had actually been finished. Olmsted quickly became disillusioned by the abandonment and collapse of Southern Reconstruction. "We have no sooner passed the point of emancipation and gained the appearance of new national unity," he wrote in 1868, "than we [are] suddenly appalled by hundreds of vortices of official meanness and corruption which betray a fearful weakness in our political system."[2]

The war changed America; it just did not change it enough. "He [Olmsted] and his friends imagined," explained the historian Geoffrey Blodgett, "that a commonwealth of free and diverse people, contained in an orderly public environment, governed by a benign and sanitary administrative state, was not only desirable but possible."[3] Olmsted would come to accept that the commonwealth envisioned in the Yosemite Report would remain largely elusive, that he had shared with many others a misplaced confidence on the finality and momentum of Union victory. Northern reformers like Olmsted, the historian Richard White observed, "assumed that once the necessary work of destruction was done, the new world would emerge. . . . They expected a self-regulating order and got near chaos."[4]

But not all was lost. Olmsted finished the 1865 Yosemite

Report barely weeks after the last Confederate forces surrendered and the Thirteenth Amendment finally took full effect across a reunited country. This seemed a momentous achievement. Since the early 1850s, the intractable struggle over Southern slavery had been an omnipresent part of his life. The antislavery cause infused his personal correspondence, his journalism, and his books and fueled social activism on behalf of beleaguered allies in West Texas and Kansas. Olmsted appreciated, just as Sarah Shaw did, that ending slavery was the keystone to achieving a broader set of social reforms. For Olmsted, victory meant that his expansive vision for "great public grounds for the free enjoyment of the people" could now emerge from under the economic and political weight of slavery and its crippling ideology of small government and entrenched opposition to national improvements.

Had anything like a Yosemite Grant or the even more radical idea of a Yellowstone National Park been introduced in the antebellum Congress, such proposals would have undoubtedly failed. Just as they feared homestead grants as "only the beginning of giving away public lands till none are left to give," Southern Democrats, committed to the unrestricted expansion of slavery, would have viewed setting aside public lands in the West for recreation and conservation with similar alarm.[5] If another grand compromise preserving slavery had been reached in 1861, or if President Lincoln had not been reelected in 1864, or the United States Army—with help from newly emancipated freedpeople—had not been victorious on the battlefield, it is likely that the development of national parks would have been stifled indefinitely along with other Republican initiatives. But times had changed, and the national government in Washington, remade and enlarged in order to win the war, now assumed new responsibilities and began to do things it had never done before.[6] For the first time public land was set aside for the benefit of all Americans, first with the Yosemite Grant, then by the establishment of Yellowstone National Park. Progress would be slow and halting, but as Olmsted's report correctly predicted, a new era of American national parks had begun.

Why then was this early history of national parks obscured in the twentieth century by historians and government officials who offered their own alternative origin stories based on totally different motivations and historical actors? The most influential of these narratives was of a legendary campfire meeting purported to have taken place at Madison Junction, on the Yellowstone Plateau, during the 1870 Washburn-Doane expedition that explored and documented the region in advance of national park legislation. This story began innocently enough, as an apocryphal tale told by Nathaniel Langford, a businessman-explorer who had been on the 1870 expedition and published an account of it in 1905.[7] Langford recounted a tale, considered by later historians to be largely his invention, of the group of scientists, artists, and leading citizens sitting around a campfire discussing the marvels of the Yellowstone region and spontaneously deciding that it should be made a national park.

The fact that neither the discussion nor the resolution occurred did not lessen the appeal of this creation myth unclouded by the complexity of politics, the social issues of the Civil War era, or the influence of corporations. The National Park Service adopted the story because, as Richard West Sellars observed, "surely the national park concept deserved a 'virgin birth'—under a night sky in the pristine American West, on a riverbank, and around a campfire, as if an evergreen cone had fallen near the fire, then heated and expanded and dropped its seed to spread around the planet."[8] By the 1960s, however, the Yellowstone park historian Aubrey Haines had already done

enough research to know that the "campfire story" was a fab-
rication—a fact that did not deter the National Park Service
from celebrating the centennial of the "national park idea" at
Madison Junction in 1972.[9] The campfire story became, in the
words of the art historian Hans Huth, a "sentimental legend,"
officially embraced by the park service well into the 1970s.[10]

As the Madison Junction story gradually lost credibility,
another creation myth arose, again involving a campfire. This
second fire was shared by John Muir and President Theodore
Roosevelt when they met during Roosevelt's visit to Yosemite in
1903. Various sources, including the agency itself, have credited
Muir and Roosevelt as visionaries responsible for launching the
national park movement and the National Park Service. Ani-
mated talkers both, Muir and Roosevelt likely discussed many
things by their campfire, including the "recession" of Yosemite
Valley and the Mariposa Grove from California back to the
United States, to become part of the larger Yosemite National
Park already established around them. But neither Muir nor
Roosevelt came up with the original idea for national parks,
and neither was responsible for the founding of the National
Park Service. National parks had existed for more than thirty
years before Roosevelt and Muir's camping trip. Despite the
fact that both Muir and Roosevelt are erroneously described
as the "fathers" of the National Park Service, the agency would
not be established until 1916—thirteen years after their campfire, and after Roosevelt had left office and Muir had died.

Roosevelt, although a great conservationist, actually had
a conflicted record when it came to national parks. On one
hand, as president he aggressively made use of the Antiquities
Act, proclaiming eighteen national monuments, in addition to
the five national parks added under his administration. On the
other, despite this enthusiasm for national parks and monu-

ments, he rejected the idea of creating a national park service. In this, Roosevelt deferred to his outspoken head of the U.S. Forest Service and trusted adviser on conservation policy, Gifford Pinchot, who steadfastly opposed the creation of a rival agency that would compete for appropriations and jurisdiction over public lands. Pinchot repeatedly proposed legislation that would have merged the national parks with the national forest system, under the presumption that his professional foresters and hydrologists were better equipped to manage them. National park advocates, fearing that such management would lead to a succession of compromising development projects, such as the Hetch Hetchy dam, relied on Congressman John Lacey, as chairman of the House Public Lands Committee, to keep Pinchot's legislative ambitions in check.

Pinchot and Roosevelt never gave up, however, and continued campaigning for their plan right up to the end of Roosevelt's administration. "I urge that all our National parks adjacent to National forests be placed completely under the control of the forest service of the Agricultural Department," Roosevelt argued in his final message to Congress, making one more pitch, "instead of leaving them as they now are, under the Interior Department and policed by the army."[11] Roosevelt and Muir are prominent figures in the history of American conservation; but the fact that the National Park Service attributes the national park system and the National Park Service largely to their influence is ironic and misleading.

Why, then, were the origin of the national park idea and early history of the agency associated for so many years with these "campfire tales"? Why did early National Park Service narratives downplay or overlook the 1865 Yosemite Report? The Yosemite Report has been a problematic document for early national park publicists for a number of reasons. First, there was the public's association of Olmsted with Central Park. The National Park Service preferred to emphasize the degree to which national parks differed from other—municipal and state—parks. The image promoted for national parks was one of high-elevation Western landscapes and pristine wilderness. This was an exclusively white, middle-class world, and the agency worked successfully to popularize the imagery that became ingrained in public consciousness. Historical associations between early national parks and Central Park were simply counterproductive to that effort. And by extension, the nineteenth-century urban parks movement—and Frederick Law Olmsted—were erased from the origin narratives and campfire tales.

Another reason the Yosemite Report was not embraced as a foundational document by the National Park Service was the perceived need to avoid the suggestion that the idea for national parks was in any way connected to the trauma and controversy of the Civil War. In the early years of the twentieth century, North-South reconciliation—between whites— and the "Lost Cause" campaign nostalgically glamorized the "Old South" and the leaders of the Confederacy. At the same time, Jim Crow policies and judicial decisions rolled back the civil rights that African Americans had gained during Reconstruction. Public memory of the war was being replaced by an alternative reality in a campaign by which, as Martin Luther King Jr. later described, "the collective mind of America became poisoned with racism and stunted with myths."[12] "By 1913 racism in America had become a cultural industry," David Blight asserted, "and twisted history a commodity. A segregated society required a segregated historical memory and a national mythology that could blunt or contain the conflict at the root of that segregation."[13] When Woodrow Wilson took office in 1912, a number of his appointees, recruited from Southern states, segregated facilities for federal workers in various departments, including the Interior, for the first time since Blacks began working for the government after the Civil War.

This was happening just as political momentum was building in Congress to establish a national park service. Supporters, seeking backing from Southern legislators and a Southern-born president, publicized a national park creation narrative unencumbered by references to emancipation, the Civil War, and Reconstruction. Giving national parks a "virgin birth" campfire narrative well served the needs of early National Park Service leaders. Historical memory was manipulated to erase reference to an activist government working on behalf of freedom, civil rights, and the remaking of the republic.

At the same time that official National Park Service histories and early annual reports distanced the national parks from potentially sensitive associations, Congress, on a parallel track, was setting aside commemorative reservations on former Civil War battlefields devoid of any references to the fight over slavery at the root of the war. In 1922, six years after the establishment of the National Park Service, the Lincoln Memorial was dedicated by President Warren Harding in a ceremony stained by the sad irony of segregated seating for event attendees.[14] "The Lincoln Memorial was presented as a shrine not to emancipation," wrote Roger Kennedy, "but to the reconciliation of North and South—reconciliation without redemption, leaving unaddressed the original sin of slavery and its lingering effects."[15]

Given the national political context in 1916, it is not surprising that there was also little mention of Olmsted; he was too closely identified with Central Park when the new national parks were being marketed as a concept born in the West; and he was too closely identified with antislavery and Union sentiment when the Civil War was being interpreted through the lens of the Lost Cause. It did not help that Olmsted was well known for writing books that effectively condemned the "Old South" and slavery. Campfire tales, on the other hand, carried no such baggage and served as a comfortable and affirming narrative. "We are a federal agency from which the public expects literal truth," protested Aubrey Haines, who questioned the veracity of the campfire story. "We should not engage in . . . propaganda." But National Park Service leadership at the time shrugged off Haines's professional scruples. "If it didn't happen," declared Lon Garrison, Midwest regional director and a former Yellowstone superintendent, "we would have been well advised to invent it. It is a perfect image. Let's use it."[16]

Does it matter today how we understand and interpret the origins of the national parks? Reconnecting the idea of the national park with the broader American park movement, the end of slavery, the Civil War, the remaking of government, and Olmsted's Yosemite Report, we believe, is an appropriate and timely historical revision. It comes at a moment when there is a serious effort to advance diversity, inclusion, and equity in the national parks.

For many years, the National Park Service has been interpreting the story of African American cavalrymen who patrolled the early national parks, but the connection of these Buffalo Soldiers with the nearly 180,000 African Americans who served in the United States Colored Troops is rarely mentioned. Connecting the national park story to emancipation and a broader struggle for freedom invites communities of color to see themselves as part of its early history. The monumental harm inflicted on generations of Native Americans, and their enduring association with national park lands, is also a part of the narrative that must be included.

For far too long, all the credit for the national parks has been vested with either mythic "rugged Western pioneers" or a "visionary" like John Muir or Theodore Roosevelt.[17] It is time to recognize those who fought for a new birth of American freedom. It is also time to revisit Olmsted's Yosemite Report and its enduring vision of popular government using its resources to improve people's lives. Olmsted's appeal for a society motivated by principles of "benevolence and equity" is keenly felt today. More than two hundred years after it was written, the report still provides a direction forward. There is an urgency to tell a refreshed national park history—and now, more than ever, it is important to get the story right.

Preliminary Report upon the Yosemite and Big Tree Grove

FREDERICK LAW OLMSTED

AUGUST 1865

It is a fact of much significance with reference to the temper and spirit which ruled the loyal people of the United States during the war of the great rebellion, that a livelier susceptibility to the influence of art was apparent, and greater progress in the manifestations of artistic talent was made, than in any similar period before in the history of the country. The great dome of the Capitol was wholly constructed during the war, and the forces of the insurgents watched it rounding upward to completion for nearly a year before they were forced from their entrenchments on the opposite bank of the Potomac; Crawford's great statue of Liberty was poised upon its summit in the year that President Lincoln proclaimed the emancipation of the slaves. Leutze's fresco of the peopling of the Pacific States, the finest work of the painter's art in the Capitol; the noble front of the Treasury building with its long colonnades of massive monoliths; the exquisite hall of the Academy of Arts; the great park of New York, and many other works of which the nation may be proud, were brought to completion during the same period. Others were carried steadily on, among them our own Capitol; many more were begun, and it will be hereafter remembered that the first organization formed solely for the cultivation of the fine arts on the Pacific side of the Globe was established in California while the people of the State were not only meeting the demands of the Government for sustaining its armies in the field but were voluntarily making liberal contributions for binding up the wounds and cheering the spirits of those who were stricken in the battles of liberty.

It was during one of the darkest hours, before Sherman had begun the march upon Atlanta or Grant his terrible movement through the Wilderness, when the paintings of Bierstadt and the photographs of Watkins, both productions of the War time, had given to the people on the Atlantic some idea of the sublimity of the Yo Semite, and of the stateliness of the neighboring Sequoia grove, that consideration was first given to the danger that such scenes might become private property and through the false taste, the caprice or the requirements of some industrial speculation of their holders; their value to posterity be injured. To secure them against this danger Congress passed an act providing that the premises should be segregated from the general domain of the public lands, and devoted forever to popular resort and recreation, under the administration of a Board of Commissioners, to serve without pecuniary compensation, to be appointed by the Executive of the State of California.

His Excellency the Governor in behalf of the State accepted the trust proposed and appointed the required Commissioners; the territory has been surveyed and the Commissioners have in several visits to it, and with much deliberation, endeavored to qualify themselves to present to the Legislature a sufficient description of the property, and well considered advice as to its future management.

The Commissioners have deemed it best to confine their attention during the year which has elapsed since their appointment to this simple duty of preparing themselves to suggest the legislative action proper to be taken, and having completed it, propose to present their resignation, in order to render as easy as possible the pursuance of any policy of management the adoption of which may be determined by the wisdom of the Legislature. The present report therefore is intended to embody as much as is practicable, the results of the labors of the Commission, which it also terminates.

As few of the Legislature can have yet visited the ground, a short account of the leading qualities of its scenery may be pardoned.

The main feature of the Yo Semite is best indicated in one word as a chasm. It is a chasm nearly a mile in average width, however, and more than ten miles in length. The central and broader part of this chasm is occupied at the bottom by a series of groves of magnificent trees, and meadows of the most varied, luxuriant and exquisite herbage, through which meanders a broad stream of the clearest water, rippling over a pebbly bottom and eddying among banks of ferns and rushes; sometimes narrowed into sparkling rapids and sometimes expanding into placid pools which reflect the wondrous heights on either side. The walls of the chasm are generally half a mile, sometimes nearly a mile in height above these meadows, and where most lofty are nearly perpendicular, sometimes over jutting. At frequent intervals, however, they are cleft, broken, terraced and sloped, and in these places, as well as everywhere upon the summit, they are overgrown by thick clusters of trees.

There is nothing strange or exotic in the character of the vegetation; most of the trees and plants, especially those of the meadow and waterside, are closely allied to and are not readily distinguished from those most common in the landscapes of the Eastern States or the midland counties of England. The stream is such a one as Shakespeare delighted in, and brings pleasing reminiscences to the traveller of the Avon or the Upper Thames.

Banks of heartsease and beds of cowslips and daisies are frequent, and thickets of alder, dogwood and willow often fringe the shores. At several points streams of water flow into the chasm, descending at one leap from five hundred to fourteen hundred feet. One small stream falls, in three closely consecutive pitches, a distance of two thousand six hundred feet, which is more than fifteen times the height of the falls of Niagara. In the spray of these falls superb rainbows are seen.

At certain points the walls of rock are ploughed in polished horizontal furrows, at others moraines of boulders and pebbles are found; both evincing the terrific force with which in past ages of the earth's history a glacier has moved down the chasm from among the adjoining peaks of the Sierras. Beyond the lofty walls still loftier mountains rise, some crowned by forests, others in simple rounded cones of light, gray granite. The climate of the region is never dry like that of the lower parts of the state of California; even when, for several months, not a drop of rain has fallen twenty miles to the westward, and the country there is parched, and all vegetation withered, the Yo Semite continues to receive frequent soft showers, and to be dressed throughout in living green.

After midsummer a light, transparent haze generally pervades the atmosphere, giving an indescribable softness and exquisite dreamy charm to the scenery, like that produced by the Indian summer of the East. Clouds gathering at this season upon the snowy peaks which rise within forty miles of each side of the chasm to a height of over twelve thousand feet, sometimes roll down over the cliffs in the afternoon, and, under the influence of the rays of the setting sun, form the most gorgeous and magnificent thunder heads. The average elevation of the ground is higher than that of the highest peak of the White Mountains, or the Alleghenies, and the air is rare and bracing; yet its temperature is never uncomfortably cool in summer, nor severe in winter.

Flowering shrubs of sweet fragrance and balmy herbs abound in the meadows, and there is everywhere a delicate odor of the prevailing foliage in the pines and cedars. The water of the streams is soft and limpid, as clear as crystal, abounds with trout and, except near its sources, is, during the heat of the summer, of an agreeable temperature for bathing. In the lower part of the valley there are copious mineral springs, the water of one of which is regarded by the aboriginal inhabitants as having remarkable curative properties. A basin still exists to which weak and sickly persons were brought for bathing. The water has not been analyzed, but that it possesses highly tonic as well as other medical qualities can be readily seen. In the neighboring mountains there are also springs strongly charged with carbonic acid gas, and said to resemble in taste the Empire Springs of Saratoga.

The other district, associated with this by the act of Congress, consists of four sections of land, about thirty miles distant from it, on which stand in the midst of a forest composed of the usual trees and shrubs of the western slopes of the Sierra Nevada, about six hundred mature trees of the giant Sequoia. Among them is one known through numerous paintings and photographs as the Grizzly Giant, which probably is the noblest tree in the world. Besides this, there are hundreds of such beauty and stateliness that, to one who moves among them in the reverent mood to which they so strongly incite the mind, it will not seem strange that intelligent travellers have declared that they would rather have passed by Niagara itself than have missed visiting this grove.

In the region intermediate between the two districts the scenery generally is of a grand character, consisting of granite mountains and a forest composed mainly of coniferous trees of great size, yet often more perfect, vigorous and luxuriant than trees of half the size ever found on the Atlantic side of the continent. It is not, however, in its grandeur or in its forest beauty that the attraction of this intermediate region consists, so much as in the more secluded charms of some of its glens, formed by mountain torrents fed from the snow banks of the higher Sierras.

These have worn deep and picturesque channels in the granite rocks, and in the moist shadows of their recesses grow tender plants of rare and peculiar loveliness. The broad parachute-like leaves of peltate saxifrage, delicate ferns, soft mosses, and the most brilliant lichens abound, and in following up the ravines, cabinet pictures open at every turn, which, while composed of materials mainly new to the artist, constantly recall the most valued sketches of Calame in the Alps and Apennines.

The difference in the elevation of different parts of the district amounts to considerably more than a mile. Owing to this difference and the great variety of exposure and other circumstances, there is a larger number of species of plants within the district than probably can be found within a similar space anywhere else on the continent. Professor Torrey, who has given the received botanical names to several hundred plants of California, states that on the space of a few acres of meadow land he found about three hundred species, and that within sight of the trail usually followed by visitors, at least six hundred may be observed, most of them being small and delicate flowering plants.

By no statement of the elements of the scenery can any idea of that scenery be given, any more than a true impression can

be conveyed of a human face by a measured account of its features. It is conceivable that any one or all of the cliffs of the Yosemite might be changed in form and color, without lessening the enjoyment which is now obtained from the scenery. Nor is this enjoyment any more essentially derived from its meadows, trees, streams, least of all can it be attributed to the cascades. These, indeed, are scarcely to be named among the elements of the scenery. They are mere incidents, of far less consequence any day of the summer than the imperceptible humidity of the atmosphere and the soil. The chasm remains when they are dry, and the scenery may be, and often is, more effective, by reason of some temporary condition of the air, of clouds, of moonlight, or of sunlight through mist or smoke, in the season when the cascades attract the least attention, than when their volume of water is largest and their roar like constant thunder.

There are falls of water elsewhere finer, there are more stupendous rocks, more beetling cliffs, there are deeper and more awful chasms, there may be as beautiful streams, as lovely meadows, there are larger trees. It is in no scene or scenes the charm consists, but in the miles of scenery where cliffs of awful height and rocks of vast magnitude and of varied and exquisite coloring, are banked and fringed and draped and shadowed by the tender foliage of noble and lovely trees and bushes, reflected from the most placid pools, and associated with the most tranquil meadows, the most playful streams, and every variety of soft and peaceful pastoral beauty.

This union of the deepest sublimity with the deepest beauty of nature, not in one feature or another, not in one part or one scene or another, not any landscape that can be framed by itself, but all around and wherever the visitor goes, constitutes the Yo Semite the greatest glory of nature.

No photograph or series of photographs, no paintings ever

prepare a visitor so that he is not taken by surprise, for could the scenes be faithfully represented the visitor is affected not only by that upon which his eye is at any moment fixed, but by all that with which on every side it is associated, and of which it is seen only as an inherent part. For the same reason no description, no measurements, no comparisons are of much value. Indeed the attention called by these to points in some definite way remarkable, by fixing the mind on mere matters of wonder or curiosity prevent the true and far more extraordinary character of the scenery from being appreciated.

It is the will of the nation as embodied in the act of Congress that this scenery shall never be private property, but that like certain defensive points upon our coast it shall be held solely for public purposes.

Two classes of considerations may be assumed to have influenced the action of Congress. The first and less important is the direct and obvious pecuniary advantage which comes to a commonwealth from the fact that it possesses objects which cannot be taken out of its domain that are attractive to travellers and the enjoyment of which is open to all. To illustrate this it is simply necessary to refer to certain cantons of the Republic of Switzerland, a commonwealth of the most industrious and frugal people in Europe. The results of all the ingenuity and labor of this people applied to the resources of wealth which they hold in common with the people of other lands has become of insignificant value compared with that which they derive from the price which travellers gladly pay for being allowed to share with them the enjoyment of the natural scenery of their mountains. These travellers alone have caused hundreds of the best inns in the world to be established and maintained among them, have given the farmers their best and almost the only market they have for their surplus products, have spread a network of rail roads and superb carriage roads, steamboat routes and telegraphic lines over the country, have contributed directly and indirectly for many years the larger part of the state revenues and all this without the exportation or abstraction from the country of anything of the slightest value to the people.

The Government of the adjoining kingdom of Bavaria undertook years ago to secure some measure of a similar source of wealth by procuring with large expenditure, artificial objects of attraction to travellers. The most beautiful garden in the natural style on the Continent of Europe was first formed for this purpose, magnificent buildings were erected, renowned artists were drawn by liberal rewards from other countries, and millions of dollars were spent in the purchase of ancient and modern works of art. The attempt thus made to secure by a vast investment of capital the advantages which Switzerland possessed by nature in its natural scenery has been so far successful that a large part if not the greater part of the profits of the Rail Roads, of the agriculture and of the commerce of the kingdom is now derived from the foreigners who have been thus attracted to Munich its capital.

That when it shall have become more accessible the Yosemite will prove an attraction of a similar character and a similar source of wealth to whole community, not only of California but of the United States, there can be no doubt. It is a significant fact that visitors have already come from Europe expressly to see it, and that a member of the Alpine Club of London having seen it in summer was not content with a single visit but returned again and spent several months in it during the inclement season of the year for the express purpose of enjoying its Winter aspect. Other foreigners and visitors from the Atlantic States have done the same, while as yet no Californian has shown a similar interest in it.

The first class of considerations referred to then as likely to have influenced the action of Congress is that of the direct pecuniary advantage to the commonwealth which under proper administration will grow out of the possession of the Yosemite, advantages which, as will hereafter be shown, might easily be lost or greatly restricted without such action.

A more important class of considerations, however, remain to be stated. These are considerations of a political duty of grave importance to which seldom if ever before has proper respect been paid by any Government in the world but the grounds of which rest on the same eternal base, of equity and benevolence with all other duties of a republican government. It is the main duty of government, if it is not the sole duty of government, to provide means of protection for all its citizens in the pursuit of happiness against the obstacles, otherwise insurmountable, which the selfishness of individuals or combinations of individuals is liable to interpose to that pursuit.

It is a scientific fact that the occasional contemplation of natural scenes of an impressive character, particularly if this contemplation occurs in connection with relief from ordinary cares, change of air and change of habits, is favorable to the health and vigor of men and especially to the health and vigor of their intellect beyond any other conditions which can be offered them, that it not only gives pleasure for the time being but increases the subsequent capacity for happiness and the means of securing happiness. The want of such occasional recreation where men and women are habitually pressed by their business or household cares often results in a class of disorders the characteristic quality of which is mental disability, sometimes taking the severe forms of softening of the brain, paralysis, palsey, monomania, or insanity, but more frequently of mental and nervous excitability, moroseness, melancholy, or irascibility, incapacitating the subject for the proper exercise of the intellectual and moral forces.

It is well established that where circumstances favor the use of such means of recreation as have been indicated, the reverse of this is true. For instance, it is a universal custom with the heads of the important departments of the British government to spend a certain period of every year on their parks and shooting grounds, or in travelling among the Alps or other mountain regions. This custom is followed by the leading lawyers, bankers, merchants and the wealthy classes generally of the Empire, among whom the average period of active business life is much greater than with the most nearly corresponding classes in our own or any other country where the same practice is not equally well established. For instance, Lord Brougham, still an active legislator, is eighty eight years old. Lord Palmerston the Prime Minister is eighty two, Earl Russell, Secretary of Foreign Affairs, is 74, and there is a corresponding prolongation of vigor among the men of business of the largest and most trying responsibility in England, as compared with those of our own country, which physicians unite in asserting is due in a very essential part to the advantage they have possessed for obtaining occasional relief from their habitual cares, and for enjoying reinvigorating recreation.

But in this country at least it is not those who have the most important responsibilities in state affairs or in commerce, who suffer most from the lack of recreation; women suffer more than men, and the agricultural class is more largely represented in our insane asylums than the professional, and for this, and other reasons, it is these classes to which the opportunity for such recreation is the greatest blessing.

If we analyze the operation of scenes of beauty upon the mind, and consider the intimate relation of the mind upon the nervous system and the whole physical economy, the action and reaction which constantly occurs between bodily and mental conditions, the reinvigoration which results from such scenes is readily comprehended. Few persons can see such scenery as that of the Yosemite and not be impressed by it in some slight degree. All not alike, all not perhaps consciously, and amongst all who are consciously impressed by it, few can give the least expression to that of which they are conscious. But there can be no doubt that all have this susceptibility, though with some it is much more dull and confused than with others.

The power of scenery to affect men is, in a large way, proportionate to the degree of their civilization and the degree in which their taste has been cultivated. Among a thousand savages there will be a much smaller number who will show the least sign of being so affected than among a thousand persons taken from a civilized community. This is only one of the many channels in which a similar distinction between civilized and savage men is to be generally observed. The whole body of the susceptibilities of civilized men and with their susceptibilities their powers, are on the whole enlarged. But as with the bodily powers, if one group of muscles is developed by exercise exclusively, and all others neglected, the result is general feebleness, so it is with the mental faculties. And men who exercise those faculties or susceptibilities of the mind which are called in play by beautiful scenery so little that they seem to be inert with them, are either in a diseased condition from excessive devotion of the mind to a limited range of interests, or their whole minds are in a savage state; that is, a state of low development. The latter class need to be drawn out generally; the former need relief from their habitual matters of interest and to be drawn out in those parts of their mental nature which have been habitually left idle and inert.

But there is a special reason why the reinvigoration of those parts which are stirred into conscious activity by natural scenery is more effective upon the general development and health than that of any other, which is this: The severe and excessive exercise of the mind which leads to the greatest fatigue and is the most wearing upon the whole constitution is almost entirely caused by application to the removal of something to be apprehended in the future, or to interests beyond those of the moment, or of the individual; to the laying up of wealth, to the preparation of something, to accomplishing something in the mind of another, and especially to small and petty details which are uninteresting in themselves and which engage the attention at all only because of the bearing they have on some general end of more importance which is seen ahead.

In the interest which natural scenery inspires there is the strongest contrast to this. It is for itself and at the moment it is enjoyed. The attention is aroused and the mind occupied without purpose, without a continuation of the common process of relating the present action, thought or perception to some future end. There is little else that has this quality so purely. There are few enjoyments with which regard for something outside and beyond the enjoyment of the moment can ordinarily be so little mixed. The pleasures of the table are irresistibly associated with the care of hunger and the repair of the bodily waste. In all social pleasures and all pleasures which are usually enjoyed in association with the social pleasure, the care for the opinion of others, or the good of others largely mingles. In the pleasures of literature, the laying up of ideas and self-improvement are purposes which cannot be kept out of view. This, however, is in very slight degree, if at all, the case with the enjoyment of the emotions caused by natural scenery. It therefore results that the enjoyment of scenery employs the mind without fatigue and yet exercises it, tranquilizes it and yet enlivens it; and thus, through the influence of the mind over the body, gives the effect of refreshing rest and reinvigoration to the whole system.

Men who are rich enough and who are sufficiently free from anxiety with regard to their wealth can and do provide places of this needed recreation for themselves. They have done so from the earliest periods known in the history of the world, for the great men of the Babylonians, the Persians and the Hebrews, had their rural retreats, as large and as luxurious as those of the aristocracy of Europe at present. There are in the islands of Great Britain and Ireland more than one thousand private parks and notable grounds devoted to luxury and recreation. The value of these grounds amounts to many millions of dollars and the cost of their annual maintenance is greater than that of the national schools; their only advantage to the commonwealth is obtained through the recreation they afford their owners (except as these extend hospitality to others) and these owners with their families number less than one in six thousand of the whole population.

The enjoyment of the choicest natural scenes in the country and the means of recreation connected with them is thus a monopoly, in a very peculiar manner, of a very few, very rich people. The great mass of society, including those to whom it would be of the greatest benefit, is excluded from it. In the nature of the case private parks can never be used by the mass of the people in any country nor by any considerable number even of the rich, except by the favor of a few, and in dependence on them.

Thus without means are taken by government to withhold them from the grasp of individuals, all places favorable in scenery to the recreation of the mind and body will be closed against the great body of the people. For the same reason that the water of rivers should be guarded against private appropriation and the use of it for the purpose of navigation and otherwise protected against obstructions, portions of natural scenery may therefore properly be guarded and cared for by government. To simply reserve them from monopoly by individuals, however, it will be obvious, is not all that is necessary. It is necessary that they should be laid open to the use of the body of the people.

The establishment by government of great public grounds for the free enjoyment of the people under certain circumstances, is thus justified and enforced as a political duty.

Such a provision, however, having regard to the whole people of a State, has never before been made and the reason it has not is evident.

It has always been the conviction of the governing classes of the old world that it is necessary that the large mass of all human communities should spend their lives in almost constant labor and that the power of enjoying beauty either of nature or of art in any high degree, requires a cultivation of certain faculties, which is impossible to these humble toilers. Hence it is thought better, so far as the recreations of the masses of a nation receive attention from their rulers, to provide artificial pleasures for them, such as theatres, parades, and promenades where they will be amused by the equipages of the rich and the animation of crowds.

It is unquestionably true that excessive and persistent devotion to sordid interests cramp and distort the power of appreciating natural beauty and destroy the love of it which the Almighty has implanted in every human being, and which is so intimately and mysteriously associated with the moral perceptions and intuitions, but it is not true that exemption from toil, much leisure, much study, much wealth are necessary to the exercise of the esthetic and contemplative faculties. It is the folly of laws which have permitted and favored the monopoly by privileged classes of many of the means supplied in nature for the gratification, exercise and education of the esthetic faculties that has caused the appearance of dullness and weakness and disease of these faculties in the mass of the subjects of kings. And it is against a limitation of the means of such education to the rich that the wise legislation of free governments must be directed. By such legislation the anticipation of the revered Downing may be realized.

> The dread of the ignorant exclusive, who has no faith in the refinement of a republic, will stand abashed in the next century, before a whole people whose system of voluntary education embraces (combined with perfect individual freedom) not only schools of rudimentary knowledge, but common enjoyments for all classes in the higher realms of art, letters, science, social recreations and enjoyments. Were our legislators but wise enough to understand, today, the destinies of the New World, the gentility of Sir Philip Sidney, made universal, would be not half so much a miracle fifty years hence in America, as the idea of a whole nation of laboring men reading and writing was, in his day, in England.

It was in accordance with these views of the destiny of the New World and the duty of the Republican Government that Congress enacted that the Yosemite should be held, guarded and managed for the free use of the whole body of the people forever, and that the care of it, and the hospitality of admitting strangers from all parts of the world to visit it and enjoy it freely, should be a duty of dignity and be committed only to a sovereign State.

The trust having been accepted, it will be the duty of the legislature, to define the responsibilities, the rights and the powers of the Commissioners, whom by the Act of Congress, it will be the duty of the Executive of the State to appoint. These must be determined by a consideration of the purposes to which the ground is to be devoted and must be simply commensurate with those purposes.

The main duty with which the Commissioners should be charged should be to give every advantage practicable to the mass of the people to benefit by that which is peculiar to this ground and which has caused Congress to treat it differently from other parts of the public domain. This peculiarity consists wholly in its natural scenery.

The first point to be kept in mind then is the preservation and maintenance as exactly as is possible of the natural scenery; the restriction, that is to say, within the narrowest limits consistent with the necessary accommodation of visitors, of all artificial constructions and the prevention of all constructions markedly inharmonious with the scenery or which would unnecessarily obscure, distort or detract from the dignity of the scenery.

In addition to the more immediate and obvious arrangements by which this duty is enforced there are two considerations which should not escape attention.

First; the value of the district is in its present condition as a museum of natural science and the danger—indeed the certainty—that without care many of the species of plants now flourishing upon it will be lost and many interesting objects be defaced or obscured if not destroyed. To illustrate these dangers, it may be stated that numbers of the native plants of large districts of the Atlantic States have almost wholly disappeared and that most of the common weeds of the farms are of foreign

origin, having choked out the native vegetation. Many of the
finer specimens of the most important tree in the scenery of the
Yosemite have been already destroyed and the proclamation
of the Governor, issued after the passage of the Act of Congress, forbidding the destruction of trees in the district, alone
prevented the establishment of a saw mill within it. Notwithstanding the proclamation many fine trees have been felled and
others girdled within a year. Indians and others have set fire to
the forests and herbage and numbers of trees have been killed
by these fires; the giant tree before referred to as probably the
noblest tree now standing on the earth has been burned completely through the bark near the ground for a distance of more
than one hundred feet of its circumference; not only have trees
been cut, hacked, barked and fired in prominent positions,
but rocks in the midst of the most picturesque natural scenery
have been broken, painted and discolored, by fires built against
them. In travelling to the Yosemite and within a few miles of
the nearest point at which it can be approached by a wheeled
vehicle, the Commissioners saw other picturesque rocks sten-
cilled over with advertisements of patent medicines and found
the walls of the Bower Cave, one of the most beautiful natural
objects in the State, already so much broken and scratched by
thoughtless visitors that it is evident that unless the practice
should be prevented not many years will pass before its natural
charm will be quite destroyed.

Second; it is important that it should be remembered that
in permitting the sacrifice of anything that would be of the
slightest value to future visitors to the convenience, bad taste,
playfulness, carelessness, or wanton destructiveness of present
visitors, we probably yield in each case the interest of uncounted
millions to the selfishness of a few individuals. It is an important
fact that as civilization advances, the interest of men in natural

scenes of sublimity and beauty increases. Where a century ago
one traveller came to enjoy the scenery of the Alps, thousands
come now and where even forty years ago one small inn accom-
modated the visitors to the White Hills of New Hampshire,
half a dozen grand hotels, each accommodating hundreds, are
now overcrowded every Summer. In the early part of the present century the summer visitors to the Highlands of Scotland
did not give business enough to support a single inn, a single
stage coach or a single guide. They now give business to several
Rail Road trains, scores of steamboats and thousands of men
and horses every day. It is but sixteen years since the Yosemite
was first seen by a white man, several visitors have since made
a journey of several thousand miles at large cost to see it, and
notwithstanding the difficulties which now interpose, hundreds
resort to it annually. Before many years if proper facilities are
offered, these hundreds will become thousands and in a century
the whole number of visitors will be counted by the millions.
An injury to the scenery so slight that it may be unheeded by
any visitor now, will be one of deplorable magnitude when its
effect upon each visitor's enjoyment is multiplied by these millions. But again, the slight harm which the few hundred visitors
of this year might do, if no care were taken to prevent it, would
not be slight if it should be repeated by millions. At some time,
therefore, laws to prevent an unjust use by individuals, of that
which is not individual but public property, must be made and
rigidly enforced. The principle of justice involved is the same
now that it will be then; such laws as this principle demands
will be more easily enforced, and there will be less hardship in
their action, if the abuses they are designed to prevent are never
allowed to become customary but are checked while they are
yet of unimportant consequence. It should, then, be made the
duty of the Commission to prevent a wanton or careless disre-

gard on the part of anyone entering the Yosemite or the Grove, of the rights of posterity as well as of contemporary visitors, and the Commission should be clothed with proper authority and given the necessary means for this purpose.

This duty of preservation is the first which falls upon the State under the Act of Congress, because the millions who are hereafter to benefit by the Act have the largest interest in it, and the largest interest should be first and most strenuously guarded.

Next to this, and for a similar reason preceding all other duties of the State in regard to this trust, is that of aiding to make this appropriation of Congress available as soon and as generally as may be economically practicable to those whom it is designed to benefit. Had Congress not thought best to depart from the usual method of dealing with the public lands in this case, it would have been practicable for one man to have bought the whole, to have appropriated it wholly to his individual pleasure or to have refused admittance to any who were unable to pay a certain price as admission fee, or as a charge for the entertainment which he would have had a monopoly of supplying. The result would have been a rich man's park, and for the present, so far as the great body of the people are concerned, it is not, and as long as the present arrangements continue, it will remain, practically, the property only of the rich.

A man travelling from Stockton to the Yosemite or the Mariposa Grove is commonly three or four days on the road at an expense of from thirty to forty dollars, and arrives in the majority of cases quite overcome with the fatigue and unaccustomed hardships of the journey. Few persons, especially few women, are able to enjoy or profit by the scenery and air for days afterwards. Meantime they remain at an expense of from

$3 to $12. per day for themselves, their guide and horses, and many leave before they have recovered from their first exhaustion and return home jaded and ill. The distance is not over one hundred miles, and with such roads and public conveyances as are found elsewhere in the State the trip might be made easily and comfortably in one day and at a cost of ten or twelve dollars. With similar facilities of transportation, the provisions and all the necessities of camping could also be supplied at moderate rates. To realize the advantages which are offered the people of the State in this gift of the Nation, therefor, the first necessity is a road from the termination of the present roads leading towards the district. At present there is no communication with it except by means of a very poor trail for a distance of nearly forty miles from the Yo Semite and twenty from the Mariposa Grove.

Besides the advantages which such a road would have in reducing the expense, time and fatigue of a visit to the tract to the whole public at once, it would also serve the important purpose of making it practicable to convey timber and other articles necessary for the accommodation of visitors into the Yo Semite from without, and thus the necessity, or the temptation, to cut down its groves and to prepare its surface for tillage would be avoided. Until a road is made it must be very difficult to prevent this. The Commissioners propose also in laying out a road to the Mariposa Grove that it shall be carried completely around it, so as to offer a barrier of bare ground to the approach of fires, which nearly every year sweep upon it from the adjoining country, and which during the last year alone have caused injuries, exemption from which it will be thought before many years would have been cheaply obtained at ten times the cost of the road.

Within the Yosemite the Commissioners propose to cause

to be constructed a double trail, which, on the completion of our approach road, may be easily made suitable for the passage of a single vehicle, and which shall enable visitors to make a complete circuit of all the broader parts of the valley and to cross the meadows at certain points, reaching all the finer points of view to which it can be carried without great expense. When carriages are introduced it is proposed that they shall be driven for the most part up one side and down the other of the valley, suitable resting places and turnouts for passing being provided at frequent intervals. The object of this arrangement is to reduce the necessity for artificial construction within the narrowest practicable limits, destroying as it must the natural conditions of the ground and presenting an unpleasant object to the eye in the midst of the scenery. The trail or narrow road could also be kept more in the shade, could take a more picturesque course, would be less dusty, and could be much more cheaply kept in repair. From this trail a few paths would also need to be formed, leading to points of view which would only be accessible to persons on foot. Several small bridges would also be required.

The Commission also propose the construction of five cabins at points in the valley conveniently near to those most frequented by visitors, especially near the foot of the cascades, but at the same time near to convenient camping places. These cabins would be let to tenants with the condition that they should have constantly open one comfortable room as a free resting place for visitors, with the proper private accommodations for women, and that they should keep constantly on hand in another room a supply of certain simple necessities for camping parties, including tents, cooking utensils and provisions; the tents and utensils to be let, and the provisions to be sold at rates to be limited by the terms of the contract.

The Commissioners ask and recommend that sums be appropriated for these and other purposes named below as follows:

For the expense already incurred in the survey and transfer of the Yosemite and Mariposa Big Tree Grove from the United States to the State of California	$2,000
For the construction of 30 miles more or less of double trail & foot paths	3,000
For the construction of Bridges	1,600
For the construction and finishing five cabins, closets, stairways, railings &c	2,000
Salary of Superintendent (2 years)	2400
For surveys, advertising, & incidentals	1000
For aid in the construction of a road	25,000
	$37,000

The Commissioners trust that after this amount shall have been expended the further necessary expenses for the management of the domain will be defrayed by the proceeds of rents and licenses which will be collected upon it.

The Yosemite yet remains to be considered as a field of study for science and art. Already students of science and artists have been attracted to it from the Atlantic States and a number of artists have at heavy expense spent the Summer in sketching the scenery. That legislation should, when practicable within certain limits, give encouragement to the pursuit of science and art has been fully recognized as a duty by this State. The pursuit of science and of art, while it tends more than any other human pursuit to the benefit of the commonwealth and the advancement of civilization, does not correspondingly put money into the hands of the pursuers. Their means are generally extremely limited. They are likely by the nature of their studies to be the best counsellors which can be had in respect to certain of the duties which will fall upon the proposed Commission, and it is right that they should if possible be honorably represented in the constitution of the Commission.

Congress has provided that the Executive shall appoint eight Commissioners, and that they shall give their service gratuitously. It is but just that the State should defray the travelling expenses necessarily incurred in the discharge of their duty. It is proposed that the allowance for this purpose shall be limited in amount to four hundred dollars per annum, for each Commissioner, or so much thereof as shall have been actually expended in travelling to and from the ground and while upon it. It is also proposed that of the eight Commissioners to be appointed by the Executive, four shall be appointed annually and that these four shall be students of Natural Science or Landscape Artists. It is advised also that in order that it may be in the power of the Governor when he sees fit to offer the slight consideration presented in the sum of $400 proposed to be allowed each Commissioner for travelling expenses as an inducement to men of scientific note and zealous artists to visit the State, that he should not necessarily be restricted in these appointments to citizens of the State. The Yosemite being a trust from the whole nation, it seems eminently proper that so much liberality in its management should be authorized.

NOTES

The following volumes of *The Papers of Frederick Law Olmsted*, under the general editorship of Charles Capen McLaughlin and Charles E. Beveridge (Baltimore: Johns Hopkins University Press), are cited in the notes as *PFLO* followed by the volume and page numbers:

Vol. 2: *Slavery and the South, 1852–1857,* ed. Charles E. Beveridge and Charles Capen McLaughlin (1981)

Vol. 3: *Creating Central Park, 1857–1861,* ed. Charles E. Beveridge and David Schuyler (1983)

Vol. 4: *Defending the Union: The Civil War and the U.S. Sanitary Commission, 1861–1863,* ed. Jane Turner Censer (1986)

Vol. 5: *The California Frontier, 1863–1865,* ed. Victoria Post Ranney (1990)

Vol. 6: *The Years of Olmsted, Vaux & Company, 1865–1874,* ed. David Schuyler and Jane Turner Censer (1992)

Vol. 7: *Parks, Politics, and Patronage, 1874–1882,* ed. Charles E. Beveridge (2007)

Vol. 8: *The Early Boston Years, 1882–1890,* ed. Ethan Carr, Amanda Gagel, and Michael Shapiro (2013)

Vol. 9: *The Last Great Projects, 1890–1895,* ed. David Schuyler, Gregory Kaliss, and Jeffrey Schlossberg (2015)

Supplementary Series (SS), Vol. 1: *Writings on Public Parks, Parkways, and Park Systems,* ed. Charles E. Beveridge and Carolyn F. Hoffman (1997)

Introduction: Three Landscapes

1. Quoted in Henry Hope Reed and Sophia Duckworth, *Central Park: A History and a Guide* (New York: Clarkson N. Potter, 1967), 33.

2. Frederick Law Olmsted, *The Cotton Kingdom: A Traveller's Observations on Cotton and Slavery in the American Slave States: Based upon Three Former Volumes of Journeys and Investigations by the Same Author,* edited with an introduction by Arthur M. Schlesinger (New York: Da Capo, 1996), 232–33.

3. Library of Congress, *American Memory Project,* "The Evolution of the Conservation Movement, 1850–1920," http://memory.loc.gov/cgi-bin/query/r?ammem/consrvbib:@FIELD(NUMBER(vm01+vm02)). The report prepared by the commissioners and written by Olmsted is known variously as the "Report on Management of Yosemite," "Yosemite and the Mariposa Grove: A Preliminary Report," and the "Preliminary Report upon the Yosemite and Big Tree Grove." For simplicity and consistency, we will refer to this document as the Yosemite Report. Olmsted's original handwritten manuscript was transcribed by his California secretary, Harry Perkins, and the Perkins document now is in the Frederick Law Olmsted Papers, Manuscript Division, Library of Congress. The first 15 pages of the 52-page document were published by the *New York Evening Post* in June 1868.

4. An Act authorizing a Grant to the State of California of the "Yo-Semite Valley" and of the Land embracing the "Mariposa Big Tree Grove" (S. 203; Public Act No. 159). For the text of laws relating to the national park system, see Hillory A. Tolson, *Laws Relating to the National Park Service and the National Parks and Monuments* (Washington, DC: GPO, 1933).

5. Letter from S. B. S. Shaw to Olmsted, August 14, 1861, United States Sanitary Commission records, box 2, 360, Manuscripts and Archives Division, New York Public Library.

6. Ibid.

1. Abolishing Slavery and Building Central Park

1. Frederick Law Olmsted, *Walks and Talks of an American Farmer in England* (1852; Amherst, MA: Library of American Landscape History, 2002).

2. Frederick Law Olmsted, *A Journey in the Seaboard Slave States: With Remarks on Their Economy* (New York: Dix & Edwards, 1856), 178.

3. See *PFLO 2*; Frederick Law Olmsted, *The Cotton Kingdom: A Traveller's Observations on Cotton and Slavery in the American Slave States* (1861), edited with an introduction by Arthur M. Schlesinger (New York: Da Capo, 1996).

4. *PFLO* 9:470.

5. Ibid.

6. *PFLO* 2:118.

7. George M. Fredrickson, *The Inner Civil War: Northern Intellectuals and the Crisis of the Union* (Urbana: University of Illinois Press, 1993), 47.

8. *PFLO* 2:118.

9. *Oration by Frederick Douglass Delivered on the Occasion of the Unveiling of the Freedmen's Monument in Memory of Abraham Lincoln* (Washington, DC: Gibson Brothers, April 14, 1876), Frederick Douglass Papers, Library of Congress, https://www.loc.gov/resource/mfd.23004.

10. *PFLO* 2:262.

11. "Hireling Labor and Slave Labor," *Southern Cultivator* 12.4 (April 1854): 105.

12. *PFLO* 2:19.

13. *PFLO* 2:6.

14. *PFLO* 3:436–41.

15. *PFLO* 2:443.

16. Olmsted to George Perkins Marsh, January 12, 1857, Frederick Law Olmsted: Chronological Letter File, box 2, University Library, American University, Washington, DC.

17. *PFLO* 2:369.

18. Laura Wood Roper, "Frederick Law Olmsted and the Western Texas Free-Soil Movement," *American Historical Review* 56.1 (October 1950): 60.

19. *PFLO* 2:382–83.

20. *PFLO* 2:414.

21. Frederick Law Olmsted Jr. and Theodora Kimball, *Forty Years of Landscape Architecture: Central Park* (1927; Cambridge, MA: MIT Press, 1973), 32–33.

22. Andrew Jackson Downing, "A Park for New York," *Horticulturalist*, August 1851, 348–49.

23. In 2017, Central Park was placed on the official U.S. Tentative List of properties potentially eligible for World Heritage designation by UNESCO. The justification was based on its importance in the history of park making and outstanding universal value: "As a work of comprehensive and picturesque landscape design on a grand scale, Central Park stands apart as a creative work that also had a great impact on the surrounding city, and on designers and urban planners influenced by its approach. A milestone in the development of landscape architecture and urban planning, it created a model that is still looked to

for urban parks, . . . made possible by the government's decision to set aside this very large space for public recreation, a striking assertion of progressive social policy."

24. *PFLO* 3:196.

25. Frederick Law Olmsted, *A Journey in the Back Country in the Winter of 1853–4*, 2 vols. (1860; New York: G. P. Putnam's Sons, 1907), 2:152.

26. George L. Scheper, "The Reformist Vision of Frederick Law Olmsted and the Poetics of Park Design," *New England Quarterly* 62.3 (September 1989): 389.

27. *PFLO* 5:385.

28. *PFLO* 3:201.

29. *PFLO* 4:506.

30. *PFLO* 3:287.

31. *PFLO* 3:342.

32. Quoted in *Proceedings of the Massachusetts Historical Society*, 2nd ser., vol. 19 (Cambridge, MA: University Press, 1905), 328.

33. Susan Schulten, *Mapping the Nation: History and Cartography in Nineteenth-Century America* (Chicago: University of Chicago Press, 2012), 133–40.

34. An image of Bache's map, partially unrolled, can be seen in the corner of Francis Bicknell Carpenter's well-known painting of President Lincoln's first reading of the Emancipation Proclamation to his cabinet.

35. *PFLO* 2:180.

36. Olmsted, *Journey in the Seaboard Slave States*, 299.

37. *PFLO* 3:36.

38. Frederick Law Olmsted, *A Report to the Secretary of War of the Operations of the Sanitary Commission and upon the Sanitary Condition of the Volunteer Army*, Sanitary Commission no. 40 (Washington, DC: McGill & Witherow, 1861), 94–95.

39. Frederick Law Olmsted, *Hospital Transports: A Memoir of the Embarkation of the Sick and Wounded from the Peninsula of Virginia in the Summer of 1862* (Boston: Ticknor & Fields, 1863), 115.

40. Katharine Prescott Wormeley, *The Other Side of War: With the Army of the Potomac* (Boston: Ticknor, 1888), 63, 10, 63.

41. George Templeton Strong, *The Diary of George Templeton Strong*, ed. Allan Nevins and Milton Halsey Thomas (Seattle: University of Washington Press, 1988), 280.

42. Carolyn L. Karcher, *The First Woman in the Republic: A Cultural Biography of Lydia Maria Child* (Durham, NC: Duke University Press, 1996), 456.

43. *PFLO* 4:286.

44. *PFLO* 4:276.
45. *PFLO* 4:130.
46. *PFLO* 4:138.
47. *PFLO* 4:40.
48. Eric Foner, *Forever Free: The Story of Emancipation and Reconstruction* (New York: Knopf, 2005), 130–31.
49. *PFLO* 3:37.
50. Horace Greeley, *An Overland Journey, from New York to San Francisco, in the Summer of 1859* (New York: C. M. Saxton, Barker, 1860), 308.
51. Thomas Starr King, *The White Hills: Their Legends, Landscape, and Poetry* (Boston: Estes & Lauriat, 1859).
52. Glenna Matthews, *The Golden State in the Civil War: Thomas Starr King, the Republican Party, and the Birth of Modern California* (New York: Cambridge University Press, 2012), 77.
53. Thomas Starr King, *A Vacation among the Sierras: Yosemite in 1860*, ed. John A. Hussey (San Francisco: Book Club of California, 1962), 37.
54. Ibid., 89.
55. Matthews, *Golden State*, 79.
56. Ralph Waldo Emerson to Thomas Starr King, November 7, 1862, King Collection—Letters, Society of California Pioneers, San Francisco.
57. Matthews, *Golden State*, 93.
58. *PFLO* 5:169.
59. Matthews, *Golden State*, 3.
60. Kevin Starr, *California: A History* (New York: Modern Library, 2005), 250.
61. *PFLO* 4:696.
62. *PFLO* 4:688.
63. *PFLO* 5:362.
64. *PFLO* 4:702.
65. *PFLO* 5:168.
66. *PFLO* 5:220.
67. Charles E. Beveridge, "The California Origins of Olmsted's Landscape Design Principles for the Semiarid American West," in *PFLO* 5:449–69.
68. Matthews, *The Golden State*, 231–33.
69. Russell M. Posner, "Thomas Starr King and the Mercy Million," *California Historical Society Quarterly* 43.4 (December 1964): 303.
70. For the text of Ward's letter and the details of the legislation, see Hans Huth, "Yosemite: The Story of an Idea," *Sierra Club Bulletin* 33.3 (March 1948): 47–78.

2. Remaking Government and the Yosemite Grant

1. Heather Cox Richardson, *To Make Men Free: A History of the Republican Party* (New York: Basic Books, 2014), 3.
2. David F. Ericson, *Slavery in the American Republic: Developing the Federal Government, 1791–1861* (Lawrence: University of Kansas Press, 2011), 12.
3. Douglas A. Irwin, *Clashing over Commerce: A History of US Trade Policy* (Chicago: University of Chicago Press, 2017), 163.
4. The new institutions were to be funded by grants of land to the states, which could sell it and use the proceeds to establish new colleges.
5. *Speech of Hon. Justin S. Morrill, of Vermont, on the Bill Granting Lands for Agricultural Colleges* (Washington, DC: Congressional Globe Office, 1858), 15.
6. U.S. Senate, "Agricultural Colleges," 35th Cong., 2nd sess., *Congressional Globe*, February 7, 1859, 851.
7. U.S. House, "Agricultural Colleges Bill," 35th Cong., 1st sess., *Congressional Globe*, April 23, 1858, 1741.
8. Ariel Ron, *Grassroots Leviathan: Agricultural Reform and the Rural North in the Slaveholding Republic* (Baltimore, MD: John Hopkins University Press, 2020), 194.
9. U.S. Senate, "Agricultural Colleges," 857.
10. The letter was Olmsted's introduction to his book *A Journey through Texas; or, A Saddle-Trip on the Southwestern Frontier* (New York: Dix, Edwards, 1857).
11. U.S. Senate, "Agricultural Colleges," 718.
12. "The 'Homestead Bill.' The Abolition 'Free Labor' Philosophy Illustrated," *Weekly Georgia Telegraph*, March 24, 1860, Digital Library of Georgia, https://gahistoricnewspapers.galileo.usg.edu/lccn/sn86077235/1860-03-24/ed-1/seq-1/.
13. Abraham Lincoln, "First Annual Message to Congress" (December 3, 1861), in *Collected Works of Abraham Lincoln*, ed. Roy P. Basler, 8 vols. (New Brunswick, NJ: Rutgers University Press, 1953), 5:49; and "Second Annual Message to Congress" (December 1, 1862), 5:537.
14. These operations were directed by a small secretive war-planning council known as the Blockade Board. The board was established to develop the military strategy to enforce the Union blockade of approximately 180 southern ports, from Virginia to Texas. The five-member board included the utilitarian director of the U.S. Coast Survey, Alexander Bache, who had in his possession the survey's 1861 slave population map. Bache was concurrently serving as vice president of

the U.S. Sanitary Commission board alongside his friend and associate Frederick Law Olmsted.

15. *PFLO* 4:235–36.

16. James Oakes, *Freedom National: Destruction of Slavery in the United States, 1861–1863* (New York: Norton, 2012), 219.

17. *PFLO* 4:517.

18. James McPherson, *Abraham Lincoln and the Second American Revolution* (New York: Oxford University Press, 1992); and David Blight, *Frederick Douglass: Prophet of Freedom* (New York: Simon & Schuster, 2018), xv.

19. David Blight, "The Civil War in American Memories at 150: Legacies in Our Own Time," keynote address presented at the annual conference of the Vermont Humanities Council, November 14–15, 2014.

20. "Speech of Hon. Elijah Babbitt, of Pennsylvania, on the Confiscation of Rebel Property," May 22, 1862, quoted in Louis P. Masur, *Lincoln's Hundred Days: The Emancipation Proclamation and the War for the Union* (Cambridge, MA: Harvard University Press, 2012), 63.

21. April 1863 testimony before American Freedmen's Inquiry Commission, set up by Secretary of War Edwin Stanton to study the transition of freedpeople from slavery to freedom. See *PFLO* 4:609–11.

22. George Perkins Marsh to Charles Eliot Norton, October 17, 1863, George Perkins Marsh Online Research Center, University of Vermont Libraries, Digital Collections, https://cdi.uvm.edu/manuscript/uvmcdi-85791.

23. Lincoln, "Second Annual Message to Congress," 537.

24. *PFLO* 4:517.

25. Blight, *Frederick Douglass,* 395.

26. *PFLO* 4:516–17.

27. Régis de Trobriand, *Four Years with the Army of the Potomac* (Boston: Ticknor, 1889), 395.

28. Abraham Lincoln, "Message to Congress in Special Session" (July 4, 1861), in *Collected Works of Abraham Lincoln,* 4:438.

29. Mark Fiege, *The Republic of Nature: An Environmental History of the United States* (Seattle: University of Washington Press, 2012), 88.

30. Leonard P. Curry, *Blueprint for Modern America: Nonmilitary Legislation of the First Civil War Congress* (Nashville, TN: Vanderbilt University Press, 1968), 247.

31. Lincoln had filled a Supreme Court vacancy with a friend of Thomas Starr King, the Californian Stephen J. Field, perhaps reflecting the crucial status of California in his larger political calculus. Years later, Field would play a key role in the Supreme Court decision against

preemption of the federal government mandate to protect Yosemite Valley.

32. U.S. Senate, "Mariposa Big Tree Grove" (debate of S.B. 203), 38th Cong., 1st sess., *Congressional Globe*, May 17, 1864, 2300–301.

33. Josiah D. Whitney, *The Yosemite Guide-Book* (Cambridge, MA: University Press, 1869), 11 available at http://www.yosemite.ca.us/library/the_yosemite_book.

34. Hans Huth, "Yosemite: The Story of an Idea," *Sierra Club Bulletin* 33.3 (March 1948): 47–78.

35. Steven Hahn, *A Nation without Borders: The United States and Its World in an Age of Civil Wars, 1830–1910* (New York: Penguin, 2017), 320–21.

36. Lincoln, "Second Annual Message to Congress," 526–27.

37. Ari Kelman, "Reconstruction in the U.S. West," in *The Reconstruction Era*, ed. Robert K. Sutton and John A. Latschar (Fort Washington, PA: National Park Service–Eastern National, 2016), 130.

38. *PFLO* 5:247.

39. Besides Olmsted, the members of the commission were Josiah Dwight Whitney, state geologist of California; William Ashburner, mining engineer and former member of the California Geological Survey; Israel Ward Raymond, originator of the bill; Erastus S. Holden, druggist and former mayor of Stockton; Alexander Deering, lawyer and former district attorney for Mariposa County; George W. Coulter, hotel keeper in Coulterville and builder of the first free trail into the Yosemite; and Galen Clark, mountaineer and first white man to discover the Mariposa Big Tree Grove. *PFLO* 5:513, n. 11, lists commission members.

40. Olmsted, Vaux & Co., "Preliminary Report to the Commissioners for Laying Out a Park in Brooklyn, New York" (1866), *PFLO* SS 1:89–90.

41. Ibid., 87.

42. *PFLO* 3:119–20, 126.

43. Roger G. Kennedy, *Wildfire and Americans: How to Save Lives, Property, and Your Tax Dollars* (New York: Hill & Wang, 2006), 133.

44. U.S. Senate, "Capitol Extension," 37th Cong., 2nd sess., *Congressional Globe*, March 25, 1862, 1349.

45. John Eaton, *Grant, Lincoln, and the Freedmen: Reminiscences of the Civil War* (New York: Longmans, Green, 1907), 89.

46. "Garibaldi and His Braves," *New York Times*, October 5, 1862.

47. Abraham Lincoln, "Address Delivered at the Dedication of the Cemetery at Gettysburg" (November 19, 1863), in *Collected Works of Abraham Lincoln*, 4:18.

48. Lincoln, "Message to Congress in Special Session" (July 4, 1861), 438.

49. Evdokia Savidou-Terrono, "For 'The Boys in Blue': The Art Galleries of the Sanitary Fairs" (PhD diss., Graduate Center, City University of New York, 2002), 18.

50. John F. Trow, *Catalogue of the Art Exhibition at the Metropolitan Fair in Aid of the U.S. Sanitary Commission* (New York, 1864).

51. In the collections of the Billings Farm & Museum and Marsh-Billings-Rockefeller National Historical Park, Woodstock, VT.

52. Richard A. Grusin, *Culture, Technology, and the Creation of America's National Parks* (Cambridge: Cambridge University Press, 2004), 17.

53. See letter to Randolph Ryer, December 2, 1863, Thomas Starr King Papers 1839–1863, Bancroft Library, University of California, Berkeley, BANC MSS C-B 304 FILM.

54. Albert Bierstadt to John Hay, August 22, 1863, John Hay Collection, Brown University Library, Providence, RI.

55. Andrew Jackson Downing, "A Park for New York," *Horticulturalist,* August 1851, 349.

56. *PFLO* 4:44.

57. *PFLO* 4:506.

58. "Our Composite Nationality" (1869), in *The Speeches of Frederick Douglass: A Critical Edition,* ed. John R. McKivigan, Julie Husband, and Heather L. Kaufman (New Haven: Yale University Press, 2018), 283, 281, 302.

59. "The Great Festival," *Nation,* July 6, 1865, 5.

60. Though Olmsted and Marsh seemed destined never to meet, they certainly knew of each other's work and corresponded. In 1857, Olmsted wrote to Marsh to enlist his support for Free-Soil settlement in Northwest Texas as way to block further western expansion of slavery. Olmsted was contacting a network of sympathetic people on the publication of his book *A Journey through Texas.*

61. George Perkins Marsh, *Man and Nature, Or, Physical Geography as Modified by Human Action,* ed. David Lowenthal (Seattle: University of Washington Press, 2003), 326, 203.

62. *PFLO* 5:354.

63. *PFLO* 5:419.

64. *PFLO* 5:402.

65. *PFLO* 5:421.

66. *PFLO* 5:403.

67. Albert D. Richardson, *Beyond the Mississippi: From the Great River to the Great Ocean* (Philadelphia: American Publishing, 1867), 435.

68. Samuel Bowles, *Across the Continent: A Summer's Journey to the Rocky Mountains, the Mormons, and the Pacific States, with Speaker*

Colfax (Springfield, MA: Samuel Bowles; New York: Hurd & Houghton, 1865), 224, 231.

69. "The Yo-Semite Valley," *New York Tribune,* June 24, 1868.
70. *PFLO* 5:36.

3. National Parks and a National Park Service

1. *PFLO* 4:26.
2. The partnership with Vaux ended in 1872, although the two would continue to collaborate later, notably on the design of the state reservation at Niagara Falls in the 1880s.
3. Dayton Duncan, *Seed of the Future: Yosemite and the Evolution of the National Park Idea* (Yosemite National Park: Yosemite Conservancy, 2013), 79.
4. Had Olmsted's design strategy for Yosemite been employed, the park would be a very different place today. Hotels, motels, restaurants, and other development would not have been built. Restrooms, some kind of stores for camping supplies, and appropriately located campgrounds would have been (although the plan did not anticipate the need for designed and structured campgrounds).
5. *PFLO* 5:466.
6. "The Yo-Semite Valley," *New York Tribune,* June 24, 1868.
7. *Hutchings v. Low,* 82 U.S. 77 (1872), *United States Reports: Cases Adjudged in the Supreme Court,* vol. 82 (Washington, DC: W. H & O. H. Morrison, 1873), 94. This case set a crucial precedent maintaining that national parks once established cannot be privatized.
8. *PFLO* 5:762.
9. *PFLO* 4:619.
10. George Perkins Marsh to Charles Eliot Norton, March 29, 1865, George Perkins Marsh Online Research Center, University of Vermont Libraries, Digital Collections, https://cdi.uvm.edu/collection /islandora-islandora771?page=2.
11. *PFLO* 6:227–28.
12. *PFLO* 6:116.
13. The Supreme Court's *Plessy v. Ferguson* decision in 1896 upheld the doctrine of "separate but equal," effectively sanctioning racial segregation until it was overturned by the Court's 1954 *Brown v. Board of Education* decision.
14. U.S. Supreme Court, "Transcription of the Judgement of the Supreme Court of the United States in *Plessy v. Ferguson,*" 163 U.S. 537 (1896), available at ourdocuments.gov.

15. Address of Frederick Billings to the American Freedmen's Union Commission of San Francisco, January 29, 1866, Billings Family Archives, Woodstock Foundation, Woodstock, VT.

16. George M. Fredrickson, *The Inner Civil War: Northern Intellectuals and the Crisis of the Union* (Urbana: University of Illinois Press, 1993), 193.

17. Garfield quoted in William Gillette, *Retreat from Reconstruction, 1869–1879* (Baton Rouge: Louisiana State University Press, 1974), 131.

18. Elaine Parsons, "Southern White Response to Reconstruction," in *The Reconstruction Era,* ed. Robert K. Sutton and John A. Latschar (Fort Washington, PA: National Park Service–Eastern National, 2016), 110.

19. Thomas H. Clark to Olmsted, July 20, 1889, *PFLO* 8:710.

20. *PFLO* 8:708–9.

21. *PFLO* 6:99.

22. Richard Franklin Bensel, *Yankee Leviathan: The Origins of Central State Authority in America, 1859–1877* (Cambridge, UK: Cambridge University Press, 1990), 2.

23. Drew Gilpin Faust, *This Republic of Suffering: Death and the American Civil War* (New York: Knopf, 2008), xiv.

24. Adam Wesley Dean, *An Agrarian Republic: Farming, Antislavery Politics, and Nature Parks in the Civil War Era* (Chapel Hill: University of North Carolina Press, 2015), 129.

25. Alfred Runte, *National Parks: The American Experience,* 4th ed. (Lanham, MD: Taylor, 2010), 39.

26. *Congressional Globe,* January 30, 1872, 697.

27. "Notes," *Nation,* March 7, 1872, 153.

28. The early vandalism of Yellowstone's geysers and other thermal features is similar to the startling burst of destruction witnessed at Joshua Tree National Park in 2019, when park staff were temporarily withdrawn during a 35-day U.S. government shutdown.

29. Richard White, *The Republic for Which It Stands: The United States during Reconstruction and the Gilded Age, 1865–1896* (New York: Oxford University Press, 2017), 115–16.

30. Lisa M. Brady, *War upon the Land: Military Strategy and the Transformation of Southern Landscapes during the American Civil War* (Athens: University of Georgia Press, 2012), 5.

31. Harold K. Steen, *The U.S. Forest Service: A History* (1976; Seattle: University of Washington Press, 1991), 26–27.

32. Frederick Law Olmsted, "Notes by Mr. Olmsted," in *Special Report of New York State Survey on the Preservation of the Scenery of Niagara Falls . . . for the Year 1879* (Albany, 1880), *PFLO* 7:474–81.

33. Among the signers was Associate Justice Stephen Field, who played

a key role in turning back the 1872 preemption challenge to Yosemite Park, and Senator Justin Morrill, champion of land-grant colleges. Former Civil War heroes signed, including Admiral David Porter, who captured New Orleans, and Montgomery Meigs, quartermaster general of the U.S. Army, who had hired Olmsted to consult on national cemeteries. Clarence King, director of the U.S. Geological Survey, who had surveyed Yosemite at Olmsted's request, also added his name, as did longtime Olmsted collaborators Henry Bellows and E. L. Godkin; literary figures Ralph Waldo Emerson, Henry Longfellow, James Russell Lowell, John Ruskin, and Oliver Wendell Holmes; scientists Asa Gray and Louis Agassiz; and artists Albert Bierstadt, Frederic Church, and Asher Durand.

34. Olmsted, "Notes by Mr. Olmsted," *PFLO* 7:474–81.

35. See Olmsted to Richard Watson Gilder, July 10, 1889.

36. See Olmsted to James H. Robb, March 30, 1889, *PFLO* 8:627–29; Olmsted to Joseph S. Fay, April 10, 1889, *PFLO* 8:629–31; F. L. Olmsted and J. B. Harrison, *Observations on the Treatment of Public Plantations, More Especially relating to the Use of the Axe* (Boston: T. R. Marvin & Son, 1889), *PFLO* 8:635–55.

37. Olmsted to Robert Underwood Johnson, October 9, 1889, *PFLO* 8, 740–42.

38. Frederick Law Olmsted, *Governmental Preservation of Natural Scenery,* March 8, 1890, *PFLO* 8:778–82.

39. Terry Gifford, ed., *John Muir: His Life and Letters and Other Writings* (Seattle: Mountaineers Books, 1996), 299.

40. Robert W. Righter, "National Monuments to National Parks: The Use of the Antiquities Act of 1906," *Western Historical Quarterly* 20.3 (August 1989): 300.

41. Steven Hahn, "What Sort of World Did the Civil War Make?," in *The World the Civil War Made,* ed. Gregory P. Downs and Kate Masur (Chapel Hill: University of North Carolina Press, 2015), 340.

42. Polly Welts Kaufman, *National Parks and the Woman's Voice: A History* (Albuquerque: University of New Mexico Press, 2006), 35.

43. J. Horace McFarland, "Are National Parks Worthwhile?" (1911), *Sierra Club Bulletin* 8.3 (January 1912): 236.

44. U.S. Congress, *Congressional Record: Proceedings and Debates of the Senate* (Washington, DC: GPO, 1892), 4124.

45. David Harmon, Francis P. McManamon, and Dwight T. Pitcaithley, *The Antiquities Act: A Century of American Archaeology, Historic Preservation, and Nature Conservation* (Tucson: University of Arizona Press, 2006), 272.

46. Richard West Sellars, "A Very Large Array: Early Federal Historic Preservation—The Antiquities Act, Mesa Verde, and the National Park Act," *Natural Resources Journal* 47 (Spring 2007): 293.

47. *Annual Reports of the Department of the Interior for the Fiscal Year Ending June 30, 1901* (Washington, DC: GPO, 1901), 349–51.

48. Ronald F. Lee, "The Story of the Antiquities Act," Archaeology Program, National Park Service, nps.gov/archeology/pubs/Lee/index .htm.

49. *Message of the President of the United States concerning Work of Interior Department and Other Matters* (Washington, DC: GPO, 1912), 8.

50. See Susan L. Klaus, "Frederick Law Olmsted, Jr.," in *Pioneers of American Landscape Design,* ed. Charles A. Birnbaum and Robin Karson (New York: McGraw Hill, 2000), 273–76.

51. Kaufman, *National Parks and the Women's Voice,* 32.

52. Olmsted Jr.'s article in the *Boston Evening Transcript* was reprinted in *Landscape Architecture* 4.2 (January 1914): 37–46.

53. Frederick Law Olmsted Jr. to the president of the Appalachian Mountain Club, January 19, 1912, quoted in Rolf Diamant, "The Olmsteds and the Development of the National Park System," in *The Master List of Design Projects of the Olmsted Firm, 1857–1979,* ed. Lucy Lawlis, Carolyn Loughlin, and Lauren Meier, 2nd ed. (Washington, DC: National Association for Olmsted Parks and National Park Service, 2008), 12.

54. McFarland, "Are National Parks Worthwhile?," 238.

55. John Muir to Kellogg family, December 27, 1913, quoted in John Warfield Simpson, *Dam! Water, Power, Politics, and Preservation in Hetch Hetchy and Yosemite* (New York: Pantheon, 2006), 176.

56. Hillory A. Tolson, *Laws relating to the National Park Service and the National Parks and Monuments* (Washington, DC: GPO, 1933), 9–10. Horace M. Albright as told to Robert Cahn, *The Birth of the National Park Service: The Founding Years, 1913–33* (Salt Lake City: Howe Brothers, 1985), 35–36; J. Horace McFarland, "The Economic Destiny of the National Parks," in U.S. Department of the Interior, *Proceedings of the National Park Conference Held in the Auditorium of the New National Museum, 1917* (Washington, DC: GPO, 1917), 104–11.

57. Frederick Law Olmsted Jr., "Vacation in the National Parks and Forests," *Landscape Architecture* 12.2 (January 1922): 107.

58. Resolutions of the American Society of Landscape Architects, *Landscape Architecture* 6.3 (April 1916): 111.

59. Stephen Mather, Horace Albright, Arno Cammerer, Newton Drury, Arthur Demaray, and Conrad Wirth. Between 1916 and 1953, Olmsted Jr. and his firm would undertake scores of planning and design projects in parks such as Acadia, Great Smoky Mountains, and Grand Canyon, and in the nation's capital.

Conclusion: Campfire Tales

1. *PFLO* 5:166.
2. *PFLO* 5:762.
3. Geoffrey Blodgett, "Frederick Law Olmsted: Landscape Architecture as Conservative Reform," *Journal of American History* 62.4 (March 1976): 889.
4. Richard White, *The Republic for Which It Stands: The United States during Reconstruction and the Gilded Age, 1865–1896* (New York: Oxford University Press, 2017), 856.
5. "The Homestead Bill," *Weekly Georgia Telegraph,* March 24, 1860, Digital Library of Georgia.
6. Leonard P. Curry, *Blueprint for America: Nonmilitary Legislation of the First Civil War Congress* (Nashville, TN: Vanderbilt University Press, 1968), 250.
7. Nathaniel Pitt Langford, *Diary of the Washburn Expedition to the Yellowstone and Firehole Rivers in the Year 1870* (Minneapolis, 1905).
8. Richard West Sellars, *Preserving Nature in the National Parks: A History* (New Haven: Yale University Press, 1997), 8.
9. Aubrey L. Haines, *The Yellowstone Story: A History of Our First National Park* (1977; Niwot: University Press of Colorado, 1996); Paul Schullery and Lee Whittlesey, *Myth and History in the Creation of Yellowstone National Park* (Lincoln: University of Nebraska Press, 2003).
10. Hans Huth, "Yosemite: The Story of an Idea," *Sierra Club Bulletin* 33.3 (March 1948): 47–78.
11. "Annual Message of the President Transmitted to Congress December 8, 1908," Office of the Historian, Department of State, https://history. state.gov/historicaldocuments/frus1908/message-of-the-president.
12. Cornell West, ed., *The Radical King: Martin Luther King Jr.* (Boston: Beacon Press, 2015), 116.
13. David Blight, *Race and Reunion: The Civil War in American Memory* (Cambridge, MA: Harvard University Press, 2001), 391.
14. With the Reorganization Act of 1933, a large number of federal prop-

erties were incorporated into the National Park Service, including battlefield reservations transferred from the War Department, and the Lincoln Memorial, transferred from the Office of Public Buildings and Public Parks of the National Capital.

15. Roger G. Kennedy, *When Art Worked: The New Deal, Art, and Democracy* (New York: Rizzoli, 2009), 316.
16. Schullery and Whittlesey, *Myth and History*, 48.
17. Ibid., 51.

ACKNOWLEDGMENTS

Our appreciation for the lifetime work of Charles E. Beveridge, the brilliant and indefatigable series editor of *The Papers of Frederick Law Olmsted*, cannot be measured. We are grateful beneficiaries of Charlie's extraordinary breadth of knowledge and the vast resources of Olmsted scholarship which he and his volume editors made so easily accessible. In particular, we are indebted to Jane Turner Censer and Victoria Post Ranney, editors of volumes 4 and 5, respectively. There is certainly a special reading room reserved in heaven for the associates of the National Association of Olmsted Parks and all the individuals and organizations that have enabled the Olmsted Papers Project to complete its work.

This book has been championed from its conception by the remarkable team at the Library of American Landscape History. In particular, we wish to thank Robin Karson, LALH founder and executive director, Jonathan Lippincott, associate director and designer, Carol Betsch, managing editor, Sarah Allaback, senior manuscript editor, and Mary Bellino, consulting editor, for all their efforts in bringing the book to fruition. We also thank the LALH Board of Directors and the many friends of LALH who generously supported the book's publication. In this regard, special thanks are owed Elizabeth Barlow Rogers and the Foundation for Landscape Studies for their early endorsement. We are also grateful for the interest and generous support of the Yosemite Conservancy and its president and CEO, Frank Dean.

The idea for this project germinated from "The Olmsteds and the National Park Service," a historic research study begun in 2014 under a cooperative agreement between the National Park Service and the Organization of American Historians (OAH). We wish to recognize and thank our third coauthor in that project, Lauren Meier, and research assistant Sharon Ricchetti. We are sincerely grateful for the support we received from the Frederick Law Olmsted National Historic Site, including Superintendent Jason Newman and our NPS project managers Alan Banks and Lee Farrow-Cook—now both retired—and from the staff of OAH, including Derek Duquette, Susan Ferentinos, the late Aidan Smith, and Paul Zwirecki.

We are singularly indebted to our manuscript readers and reviewers, including Judith Benedict, Joseph Corn, David Harmon, Dwight Pitcaithley, and John Reynolds. We deeply appreciate their discerning insights and unflagging encouragement. Many libraries and archives not only made materials available to us but went out of their way to be helpful. In particular, we want to recognize Tal Nadan at the New York Public Library Brooke Russell Astor Reading Room for Rare Books and Manuscripts; Lars Johnson at the Bancroft Library of the University of California and its collections staff curating the Thomas Starr King Papers; Marianne Zephir at the Billings Farm & Museum Archives; Ryan Polk at Marsh-Billings-Rockefeller National Historical Park; Jeffrey Marshall at the University of Vermont Silver Special Collections Library; and the staff of the Olmsted Archives at the Frederick Law Olmsted National Historic Site.

Greg Moore, Golden Gate National Parks Conservancy CEO emeritus, a most generous and resourceful friend, opened many doors for us in California. There are other good people who cheered on this undertaking, including Wanda Corn, Dennis Duncan, John Elder, Peter Gilbert, Bethann Johnson, Dave Johnson, Richard Larson, Victoria Larson, Peter Lukacic, Christina Marts, Sandra Mika, Dan Nadenicek, J. T. Reynolds, Ellen Wolfe, and Edward Zlotkowski, and, last but not least, a most patient listener, editor, and critic, Nora Mitchell, who never lost sight of the book's audience and purpose—and the importance of finishing it.

Olmsted and Yosemite was made possible with the generous support of the following:

Susan L. Klaus

Foundation For Landscape Studies
Yosemite Conservancy

Friends of Fairsted

Nancy G. Frederick

The Lauren Belfer and Michael
    Marissen Fund, Vanguard
    Charitable
Nancy Carol Carter
Burks Hamner
Joseph Hibbard, ASLA
Michael and Evelyn Jefcoat
Keith N. Morgan, FSAH
Lloyd P. Zuckerberg

Anonymous
Mr. and Mrs. Craig Barrow III
George W. Curry, FASLA, in honor
    of Robert Page
Jeffrey J. Dyer
Linda Lee Jewell, FASLA
David R. LePere and Thomas H.
    Woodward
Dennis C. McGlade, ASLA
Nancy Newcomb and John
    Hargraves
Peter Pennoyer, AIA, Peter
    Pennoyer Architects
San Gabriel Nursery & Florist, in
    memory of Fred Waichi and
    Mitoko Yoshimura
David W. White
Dana and Joe Woody

Donald Albrecht
Karen Bartholomew
Philip and Shelley Belling
Richard Bergmann, FAIA, ASLA
Laura Louise Breyer
Josephine Bush, in memory of Ann
    D. Wilhite
Timothy Callis
Jay Cantor
Dr. and Mrs. Charles Carroll IV
Nancy Carol Carter
Staci Catron, Atlanta History
    Center
John Clayton and Will Jolley
David B. Coleman
Kelly Comras, FASLA
James C. Differding, ASLA
Terese D'Urso
Derrick Eichelberger, ASLA
Alan Emmet
Elsbeth T. Falk
Nancy Fee, in honor of Dr. Mark
    Brack and in memory of
    Florence Fee Smith
Ian Firth, FASLA
Esley Hamilton
Margarete R. Harvey, ASLA
Marian Hill
Heidi Hohmann, ASLA
Cheryl and Kevin Hurley, in
    memory of Ann and Clayton
    Wilhite
David Kamp, FASLA
Sidney I. Landau
Lucy Lawliss, ASLA
Richard Longstreth
Richard Margolis
Hugh C. Miller, FAIA

Douglas Moreland
Darrel G. Morrison, FASLA
Mary Eugenia Myer
Audrey Nevins and John
    McNamara
Carl R. Nold
Thomas M. Paine, ASLA
Dr. and Mrs. W. Scott Peterson,
    Connecticut Community
    Foundation
Anne Neal Petri
Jon Powell, ASLA, and Jeri
    Deneen
Leslie and Dennis Power
Dr. and Mrs. Richard Rhoda

Barbara Robinson, Widgeon Point
    Foundation, in memory of
    John R. Robinson
Elizabeth Barlow Rogers
Karen Sebastian, ASLA
Frances Shedd-Fisher
Fred Simon, ASLA
Frederick Steiner
Catherine M. Stone Fund
Todd and Mary Ishihara Swanton
Nancy B. Taylor
Jeannette G. Walker
Peter Walker, FASLA
Robert Whitlock
Ted Wolff

INDEX